LEARNING THE SKILLS OF PEACEMAKING

AN ACT...
FOR ELE... ...AGE CHILDREN
...TING,
...LICT

... K. Gandhi

LEARNING THE SKILLS OF PEACEMAKING

AN ACTIVITY GUIDE FOR
ELEMENTARY-AGE CHILDREN
ON COMMUNICATING,
COOPERATING,
RESOLVING CONFLICT

by Naomi Drew

Foreword by Yogesh K. Gandhi

Jalmar Press
Rolling Hills Estates, California

WHAT OTHERS HAVE TO SAY...

"I am deeply touched that my book *Human Options* figured in your decision to create *Learning the Skills of Peacemaking,* and I offer you every good wish with this important undertaking."

NORMAN COUSINS

"I want to express my sincere admiration and support for your excellent program....I wish that we could see similar learnings going on in every classroom at every level."

JOANN B. LIPSHIRES
New Jersey Education Association

"Learning the Skills of Peacemaking addresses the problems of peace and negotiation precisely where the destinies of the superpowers are now being formulated—in the minds and souls of young people. The adoption of this remarkable educational program will surely be a positive force in international relations in years to come."

DAVID LANDAU
Author of *Kissinger: The Uses of Power*

"This peacemaking program will have an immediate impact on the lives of the children involved. Naomi Drew has not only articulated noble goals but has devised psychologically sound means to meet those goals."

BEATRICE GROSS
Author of *The Great School Debate: Which Way for American Education*

"The material is thoughtful, sensitive, and child-centered. It seems to me to be an intelligent, practical approach to a complex topic."

PROFESSOR VINCENT R. ROGERS
Department of Education, University of Connecticut

"How far we have come in peace education! Naomi Drew's book is packed full of exciting and usable new ideas and activities."

PRISCILLA PRUTZMAN
Author, *The Friendly Classroom for a Small Planet*

"Global peace begins with you. *Learning the Skills of Peacemaking* develops this fundamental concept in fifty-six lessons that personalize each individual's responsibility for respecting human differences, disavowing violence, and finding alternative means of resolving conflict. If this curriculum was a required course in every elementary school in every country, we would see world peace in our children's lifetime."

LETTY COTTIN POGREBIN
Author of *Family Politics, Growing Up Free,* and *Among Friends.* Also founding editor of *Ms.* magazine.

"There is a need to teach friendship and cooperation at the earliest level. My son has benefited from the understandings and concepts of the . . . program."

MRS. SUSAN GRAZIANO
Parent of Student Participant

"Without question, your program is the most powerful I have ever participated in as an educator. You rekindled in me my purpose as a teacher to assist children in living in love and peace with themselves, their families, and friends and to take that attitude responsibly out into the world. Through your program, I have also experienced a sense of dignity as a teacher that had been slowly falling away through the years."

GAIL WEITZ
Third Grade Teacher

Published by Jalmar Press
45 Hitching Post Drive, Building 2
Rolling Hills Estates, California 90274

Designer: Susan Brewer
Illustrator: Jacqueline Lamer Lockwood

ISBN: 0-915190-46-X

Library of Congress Number: 87–81609
Printed in the United States of America
10 9 8 7 6 5

"Would that I could be the peacemaker in your soul, that I might turn the discord and the rivalry of your elements into oneness and melody. But how shall I, unless you yourselves be also the peacemakers . . ."

Kahlil Gibran

This book is dedicated to: my two children, Michael and Timmy Drew, whose lives have taught me to search for the meaning of peace for all human life,

and

to Norman Cousins, whose ideas and commitment to the "larger world" created the impetus for this book,

and

to my parents Molly and Philip Schreiber, without whom none of this would be possible.

CONTENTS

LEARNING THE SKILLS OF PEACEMAKING
AN ACTIVITY GUIDE FOR ELEMENTARY-AGE CHILDREN
ON COMMUNICATING/COOPERATING/RESOLVING CONFLICT

SPECIAL THANKS

I'd like to thank the following people without whom the completion of this book and all of our work would not have been possible:

Michael Dee for enabling me to step out of the classroom and dedicate three years of my life to this work.

Marguerite Chandler for providing all of the many levels of support she has given to help this program grow and move forward.

Dr. Samuel H. McMillan, Jr., of The National Foundation for the Improvement of Education, for all his support and assistance.

Phyllis Yannetta for her loving, loyal, and continuous support, and for the hours of time she put into the preparation of this book.

Gail Weitz for her loving support and for the vital input she gave toward the shaping of new ideas for this book.

Jan Lovelady for her patience, support, and enthusiasm in the editing of this book.

Suzanne Mikesell for completing the editing of this book and for her thoughtful and perceptive comments.

Hal Sobel for his expert input as validator of the pilot program.

Brad Winch for his constant encouragement and helpfulness.

Therese LaMontagne for tirelessly typing the bulk of the manuscript.

My 1983-84 first grade class at the Clark Mills School in Manalapan-Englishtown who taught me more than they could ever imagine.

SPECIAL ACKNOWLEDGMENTS GO TO:

Heather Diaforli who created the beautiful painting that appears on the cover of this book.

AT&T, National Starch & Chemical, the Squibb Corporation, and the Edmar Corporation for providing grants to fund the pilot study.

The National Foundation for the Improvement of Education for their invaluable assistance in the research and development phase of this program.

I'd also like to acknowledge the following people as contributors to the lesson ideas in this book: Carole Messersmith, Pat Hoert- doerfer, Julia Greene, Judy Lepore, Gail Weitz, Linda Herman, and Priscilla Snow Algava.

Very special thanks to the Board of Partners in Peacemaking for their love, support, and enthusiasm:

Michael Dee, Bruce McCracken, Peter Jenkins, Andy Algava, Sandy Silverstone, Joana Reigel, Betty Levin, Richard Burke and Gail Weitz.

FOREWORD

At the core of this book is a simple but far-reaching idea: Peace can be achieved through individual effort and commitment to nonviolence. Peacemaking and conflict resolution techniques are not new concepts, but have emerged out of a necessity for solving global, institutional, and interpersonal disputes.

We have come to think of these resources as useful primarily to adults. *Learning the Skills of Peacemaking* demonstrates the importance of targeting our efforts toward another population: children. It is in childhood that our sense of self is born, our world view is formed, and our methods of dealing with frustration and conflict are learned. It is also during this time that our ideals are inspired. If as children we learn to be peaceful—optimistic that we can achieve our dreams—as adults we can spend our time contributing fully to society rather than undoing unproductive habits.

We know from research that the influence of the family on children's psychological and social development is great. Education, too, plays a key role in shaping children's attitudes. The classroom is a legitimate arena for engaging children in the process of peacemaking. In compiling this guide, Naomi Drew draws upon her experience as an educator, researcher, and parent. She provides concrete lesson plans and specific instruction in peacemaking techniques that foster self-respect, respect for others, and effective communication. She underscores the need to create a safe and nurturing learning environment that allows children to express their concerns and to arrive at creative and spontaneous solutions. Through understanding, flexibility, and negotiation, children learn to resolve problems assertively, without violence.

But the real challenge presented to educators and to us all is to become what we teach. The example that we set tells children more about how we really feel and think than words do. I am reminded here of a story in which a mother was discouraged because of her son's resistance to changing his poor eating habits. Knowing his admiration for Mahatma Gandhi, she travelled 300 miles on foot with her son in the hope that Mahatma would counsel him not to eat sugar. When they arrived, Mahatma told them to return in two weeks. Despite her weariness and disappointment, she obeyed. Upon their return, Mahatma met with her son and it is said that out of devotion to this great leader, the child changed his ways. The mother, however, asked Mahatma why he chose not to speak with her son on the first visit. It is said that Mahatma replied, "Two weeks ago I was eating sugar."

As children begin to understand and integrate peacemaking techniques, it then becomes appropriate to extend these lessons to address global issues. Children are given the opportunity to explore the similarities and differences in customs, attitudes, and policies of other nations and to envision a world at peace. Through clarity about our goal and perseverance in our commitment to effect peace, we can dispel the discouragement that comes from the belief that violence and war are inevitable. As we begin to disseminate information on innovative and peaceful approaches to conflict resolution and to share our knowledge, we will make the great longing for world peace a reality.

Learning the Skills of Peacemaking is an integral part of this process.

Yogesh K. Gandhi, Founder
Gandhi Memorial International Foundation

THE LIGHT-BEARERS

by Jessica Hirst, age 11

Light, cascading down
Turning rainbow colors
Over, under, through almost everything
Obstructions are overcome
Light washes over beings
Some greedily take it in
And keep it for their own pleasure
Many try to use it positively, help it grow
They try, but they do not have the knowledge
A few accept it, have knowledge to use it
They teach others
These few are the Light-Bearers
To carry the light for others
To give Light to beings
A sad child
A despairing youth
A weary elder
All are taught
The sun will rise again
Have hope, hold it tight
Be Light-Bearers
Help hurt ones, before souls flee
Overcome selfishness, cruelty
Save yourselves from self-destruction
Light, cascading down
Turning rainbow colors
Into the welcoming arms
Of the Light-Bearers

PREFACE

If we are to reach real peace in the world we shall have to begin with children; and if they will grow up in their natural innocence, we won't have to struggle; we won't have to pass fruitless ideal resolutions, but we shall go from love to love and peace to peace, until at last all the corners of the world are covered with that peace and love for which consciously or unconsciously the whole world is hungering.

— Gandhi

During the eleven years that I taught elementary school, I came to realize that the system educates children about reading, language, math, and other subjects, but not about the most important one of all: how to interact with each other and the world at large. I began to research the issues that most concern today's children, and what I found was that young people have deep fears about the future.

I also learned that when students are given a chance to discuss the future, a future free of fear, and how they might help bring about such a future, they become more hopeful. They begin to see the possibility of a role for themselves in creating a peaceful future.

I felt a strong need for a program that would actually teach the skills of peacemaking in the same way math, reading, and spelling are taught. Such a program would demonstrate that peacemaking, like math or reading, is logical, practical, invaluable.

I expanded the program I first piloted in my own school over the years and it is now used by schools and communities in many different states. In fact, the program has gained so much recognition that it was presented to members of President Reagan's staff at the White House.

What began it all was an in-depth examination of the following questions:

- How does education prepare young people for the future when so many feel that there will be no future?

- Does education offer youth values and a sense of responsibility to the world beyond themselves or just training in basic skills?

- Does education offer children good reasons to live and hope?

- Are young people learning the skills they'll need to deal with a rapidly changing technology and an expanding concept of the world?

- Does education empower youth to begin shaping the future? If not, how can it begin to do this?

Learning the Skills of Peacemaking addresses these questions. It teaches specific skills as well as a general problem-solving process by which children can begin to create the kind of future we all want: a peaceful one. It demonstrates that cooperation is not only achievable in home and at school, it may actually be more natural for us than conflict. Conflict, while always present in life, does not determine its course. Generally, we prefer to get along with each other, to work out our differences.

Ask your students or your children which kind of atmosphere they prefer—one of anger and upset, or one of peacefulness and harmony? The choice is evident. We prefer harmony, but we are not always sure how to achieve it. Creating an atmosphere of acceptance and peace is possible, but maintaining it takes enormous commitment, practice, and the willingness to leave old habits behind. Choosing conciliation over opposition is a constant challenge.

An atmosphere of peacefulness and compromise includes the following elements:

- cooperation

- calmness

- willingness to work out differences

- ability to work collaboratively to solve problems

- love and acceptance

- the ability to say, "I'm human. I've made a mistake. I'll try again."

An atmosphere of peacefulness supports the well-being of all parties involved. It's a dynamic atmosphere in which the old ways are questioned as the new ways evolve.

Peace begins with the individual commitment to having a better world. Education can foster this commitment. You, as the teacher, are able to take the first step in imparting this dynamic. Your way of dealing with discipline, resolving conflicts, affirming each child's value, and pointing out his or her connections to the world forms the base for a commitment to peace.

Learning the Skills of Peacemaking was designed to be used as a springboard for positive interactions with your students. Integrate the texture of each lesson into the classroom atmosphere. By using the techniques in this book throughout the day, you will create a calm, cooperative, peaceful classroom.

Peace is more than the absence of war. It is an active, collaborative process by which human beings take direct responsibility for dealing with the problems they face.

Naomi Drew

INTRODUCTION

Learning the Skills of Peacemaking is a guide for teachers, parents, and other caregivers who wish to bring the skills of peacemaking to life for children. It focuses on four major concepts:

- Accepting self and others
- Communicating effectively
- Resolving conflicts
- Understanding intercultural differences

Peacemaking skills are presented in three "stages," with each stage integrating lessons in these four concept areas. There are fifty-six lessons in all. Stage I is "Peace Begins with Me," Stage II is "Integrating Peacemaking," and Stage III is "Exploring Our Roots and Interconnectedness." Each stage is multi-graded. Although I recommend some of the lessons for particular grade levels, please adapt them to your own class situation even if your students don't fall into the suggested grade level range.

Peruse the entire guide before you begin to teach it, to see which lessons best suit your classroom needs. Each class is different. Your creativity and flexibility in the use of this book will make it more meaningful to your children. Don't be afraid to do the lessons in a different order, either. Just make sure to introduce any new ideas or terminology carefully. Some of the concepts will be completely new to your students.

Learning the Skills of Peacemaking uses many methods to teach peacemaking skills, such as: playacting, creative writing, story-reading, music, the arts, and classroom discussion. The lessons can be used approximately twice a week to enrich both the social studies and language arts programs. However, since the concepts and values in each lesson are meant to be woven into all your daily interactions, use them regularly throughout the week to fully nurture a classroom atmosphere of peacemaking.

For example, some of the imagery exercises might be done first thing in the morning to set the tone for the day. The conflict resolution guidelines can be applied whenever a stressful situation arises. "Showcase" conflict situations as they occur, mediating them through the use of the Win/Win Guidelines, and engage the entire class in problem solving (see the next chapter for a discussion of The Win/Win Guidelines and the concept of "showcasing.") Occasionally stopping whatever you are doing to resolve a conflict and explaining that this is part of the process of peacemaking can have a tremendous impact.

Remember, the basic concepts in *Learning the Skills of Peacemaking* are interwoven in each stage. As the children focus on peacemaking in their lives, they begin to see how these skills can be applied to the world beyond themselves. Thus the lessons become more abstract as they go along.

You will find current events infused into each section to highlight the connection between individual acts and world events. For example, at one point when the children are learning conflict resolution skills, they examine a selected current event article relating to a conflict situation. They are asked: "How can this situation be resolved through the use of conflict resolution skills?" Such a query broadens their perspective and guides them to recognize that they are a part of the larger world—community, nation, and earth—as well as of the smaller one—home, neighborhood, and school.

Children discover that they belong to the whole human family, that they are connected in many ways to other people throughout the world. More importantly, they learn that peace begins with each person, that the same techniques that average people use to work out problems can be used by world leaders. This is not to over-simplify the complexities of today's international conflicts, but to show that individuals, regardless of title or position, have options they can pursue to resolve differences.

MAKING
PARENTS YOUR PARTNERS

When I first started developing the peace-making lessons in my 1983-84 first grade class, parents of my students became curious. I began receiving calls, like this one from Todd's mother: "Mrs. Drew, what are you doing with Todd? He's started acting differently. He seems to be more willing to work out problems and he's not fighting with his brother as much. When I asked him why the sudden change, he said, 'We're learning how to be peacemakers in our school. Our teacher's showing us ways we can get along better.' Could you tell me about what you're doing? I'd like to learn it, too."

Another mom said: "Michael's Sunday school teacher said that Michael has developed an added sensitivity to others that's rare in children his age. He asked me what I was doing to bring this about. I told him that Michael was doing a special program in school. Could you tell me more about it?"

After several conversations, I invited the parents to come in and observe or participate in lessons. I also held some after-school meetings. This was effective on several levels: it helped create a greater partnership with the parents; it provided hands-on information and techniques; and it enabled parents to understand what we were doing in school so they could reinforce the ideas at home.

Holding meetings for parents will help you build a partnership with them. September is a good time to begin. An after-school coffee or an evening meeting will provide the opportunity to show them this guide and introduce its concepts and goals. A visual display such as the "Me Mobiles" from Lesson 2 is a great conversation piece. Parents always enjoy seeing their children's work displayed, especially projects of such a personal nature as the mobiles.

A step beyond observation is to actually include parents in some of the lessons. Many lessons lend themselves to "audiences," oral report presentations in particular. Any opportunity to involve parents supports their efforts to reinforce at home the skills their children are learning at school.

THE HIERARCHY
OF PEACEMAKING

Picture yourself holding up a tall ladder. You are at the base. If you let go, the ladder topples. If your grip is firm, the ladder is steady. So it is with peacemaking. Peace starts with each individual. It emerges first from within and then manifests itself most basically in the way people feel about themselves. I reiterate the importance of a positive self-concept in this book because this is the critical key to becoming a successful peacemaker. Self-concept influences our every action, interaction, and reaction.

With a positive self-image, you are ready to go up to the next rung on the ladder—one-to-one interactions. This level encompasses interpersonal relationships—those between friends, teacher and student, brother and sister, neighbors, etc. At this place on the ladder we challenge students to communicate effectively, resolve conflicts positively, and solve problems collaboratively.

Relationships in small groups follow—family, neighborhood, school, religious groups, civic groups, etc. Peacemaking moves up to en-compass greater numbers of people and more complex interactions. Shifting for a moment to look back, down to the source, become aware that it is the inner landscape that largely determines how you will relate in groups. When you feel whole and at peace within, you can relate to others more effectively. When you feel unworthy, inadequate, or troubled, you will manifest such emotions in the way you deal with and perceive others. Picture the children in your class. Almost inevitably those who act out or are withdrawn from others are children who don't feel good about themselves.

As you continue to move up the ladder, you encounter larger and larger groups. You step up to the community, then the state, the nation, the hemisphere, and finally the world. How you perceive and relate to the world depends on how you relate to yourself. Ask yourself:

- How can I serve the world beyond myself?

- How can I best relate to the people around me?

- How can I reach out beyond what looks like my small sphere of influence into a larger sphere?

- How can I make a difference in the world?

REPEATING THE LESSONS

Just as number facts need to be reviewed periodically, so it is with peacemaking skills. These lessons are designed to be repeated year after year, with variations supplied by each teacher. If you are teaching third grade, for example, and your class did most of the peacemaking lessons in second grade, I would suggest doing the lessons again but modifying them in your own way. Have a class discussion. Tell the children that because their growth and experiences during the past year provided them with new insights and understandings, their present responses to the lessons will be somewhat different. Let the children know that repeating lessons reinforces their changing attitudes and behaviors.

You will need to be creative in this effort. You can vary the activities and discussions but keep the objectives in mind when doing so. Brainstorm with other teachers and find out

what new ideas they've discovered in teaching peacemaking skills. I would be delighted to see any new activities and lessons you come up with. My address is listed at the end of the chapter, "The Win/Win Guidelines."

Remember, repetition is critical to a child's absorption of new understandings. Change takes time, practice, and adaptation, but it should be enjoyable, too. Making the lessons fun will enhance your children's grasp of the material.

IMAGING

The use of "imaging" or creative visualization is employed throughout the lessons in this guide. Imaging has many applications, particularly:

—calming children, helping them to become focused at the start of many lessons;

—envisioning solutions to conflicts and other problems;

—envisioning what kind of school, country, and world each person wants to have.

Many people value the benefits of imagery. Norman Vincent Peale called it one of the great principles of creative living. He cautioned, however, that "imaging is not a magic formula that simply, by some kind of mental trick, brings results. In an amazing way, it does open doors to problem solving and goal achievement. But once those doors are open there must be discipline, determination, patience, and persistence if problems are to be solved or if dreams are to become a reality."[1]

Dr. Peale tells how he first learned of this technique from Theodore Roosevelt. As a young minister, Peale was terrified of public speaking yet he had to address a crowd of fifty thousand. Roosevelt was also scheduled to speak and was aware of Peale's fear. He said,

"Get up there and talk, and I'm going to sit right behind you and visualize you loving these people, helping them, and holding them spellbound. I have a picture of how it will happen."

Peale goes on to say that the image Roosevelt held for him actually manifested, and his speech was a huge success. Roosevelt's response was: "Now you see that if you think you can, or somebody who believes in you thinks you can, then you can."[2]

Roosevelt's statement applies most poignantly to the way teachers can hold the vision of success, cooperation, and achievement for their students. Beyond this, imagine the visions you can hold for a peaceful future for your students and for the world's students.

Psychology Today sheds light on the process of imagery, saying "We all have inner vision that enables us to create scenes that our outer vision has never beheld....With it, a sixteen-year-old Albert Einstein was able to picture himself aboard a sunbeam traveling at the speed of light thereby developing the seminal idea of his theory of relativity."[3]

Talking about the continued evolution of our species, Dr. Jonas Salk once noted that human consciousness, and hence all future growth, achievement, and relationships, begins with..."an idea generated in the human mind."[4] Such ideas are developed in our creative images.

Problem solving on many different levels can be addressed through imagery. In *Experiences in Visual Thinking*, Bob McKim states, "When problems are imagined in a tangible, seeable way, solutions come to mind with more force, more variety, more detail."[5]

The future starts in today's images. The applications are limitless.

THE IMPORTANCE OF TEACHING PEACEMAKING SKILLS

I have discovered that inevitably something starts to "shift" as teachers and children internalize the concepts of peacemaking presented in this book. Here is an example shared by one teacher:

"The room was so quiet you could hear your own breathing. The children were seated on the floor in a circle, legs crossed. Each child's eyes were closed. The children were asked to envision the world just as they would want it to be. They were asked to imagine people of all races, religions, colors, and nationalities getting along. How would the world look? How would it be different from the way it is now? How would they feel if the world were as they envisioned it?

"The children sat for a few moments in deep concentration and silence. One by one they began to open their eyes. One boy said, 'I pictured black and white children playing together.' A little girl said, 'I pictured a world with no more wars, where people learned to work out their differences together.'"

Be aware that children, as well as adults, may resist the shift toward peacemaking in a non-peaceful world. Some teachers have said,

"Sometimes children come to me and say, 'I'm not a peacemaker because there are times I still fight,' or, 'Why should I try to get along with others, when they don't try to get along with me?'" Expect such questions—they are part of the process of integrating peacemaking skills. You will challenge children's perceptions as well as their actions in this program, and change takes time.

Be patient and be aware of the small, gradual changes as they evolve. As one teacher said after completing *Learning the Skills of Peacemaking*, "Some of my children still fight, but now they've begun to take responsibility for their actions."

Footnotes
[1] Norman Vincent Peale, "Make Your Dreams Come True," *Reader's Digest*, August, 1982, pp.155-160.
[2] *Ibid.*
[3] Guillen, "Mind Viewers," *Psychology Today*, May, 1984, pp.73-74.
[4] Peter Stoker, "A Conversation with Jonas Salk," *Psychology Today*, March, 1983, pp.51-55.
[5] Stewart, "Teachers Aim at Turning Loose the Mind's Eyes," *Smithsonian Magazine*, August, 1985, pp.44-55.

USING THIS GUIDE: NOTES FOR TEACHERS AND PARENTS

Although parents as well as teachers will be using this guide, I refer to "classroom" and "students" rather than "family" and "children" for simplicity's sake. Please adapt the instructions for your use with individuals or groups, as appropriate.

BEGIN WITH A DISCUSSION:

Tell the class about your own commitment to having a peaceful class. Give your reasons for caring about this. Discuss them with the group. Discuss students' feelings and responses, along the following lines:

"What kind of class do you want to have?"

"How do you want to be treated by your classmates?"

"What do you think are the qualities of a peaceful class?"

Make a preliminary chart of qualities and hang it up. Use it as a beginning, a starting point. The list of qualities will grow. Have each class member participate in the completion of this chart. Review it together from time to time to reinforce the concepts. Complete your discussion with the following questions:

- "How would our class be if we all did our very best to get along?"

- "How would the world be different if everybody were committed to peace and knew how to make it a reality?"

- What does it mean when we say, "Peace begins with you?"

Don't be surprised if your students voice feelings of despair, resignation, or apathy during the discussion. Allow this to happen and allow your own negative feelings to surface as well. This is a crucial part of the process. As you become more and more involved in peace making, you'll begin to recognize the unworkability of old patterns or solutions. Sometimes this is manifested as a lack of faith in new solutions.

For instance, you might think, "This can't work. Human nature just isn't conducive to putting aside differences and agreeably resolving conflict." If this happens, know that the reverse side of this feeling is a feeling of possibility. Giving in to hopelessness renders us powerless. Your faith in the process is the catalyst—through it you will discover that slowly you can develop harmony and cooperation in school and at home. *It takes time.* Remember this, and be patient.

Daily interactions are usually the first demonstration of one's commitment to peace. In my own family, we had an extended discussion about this. One of the questions that came up was, "How can we expect nations to get along if we can't get along in our own home?" The realization that followed was, if we could find ways to work out differences and get along in our own home, then perhaps other people could do it, too. We talked about the fact that people hurt each other all the time throughout the world, but if we wanted a better, safer world, then it had to first start at home.

My children began to see that we all must take responsibility for peacemaking. Often it's much easier to place the blame for conflict on others or on circumstances. Looking within and discovering our own responsibility in each conflict goes against many ingrained behaviors. But that's precisely where authentic problem solving and peacemaking begin.

Bringing forth your students' vision and commitment before teaching the conflict resolution process is extremely important. Vision and commitment are the most vital elements in any peacemaking effort. Without them, the process is hollow and meaningless. *A commitment is a promise we make to ourselves and others that we keep no matter what.* It's not based on circumstances; it does not depend on the actions of others. A commitment is rooted within each person and is entirely dependent upon his or her willingness to generate it.

Ask your children, "Are you willing to be committed to working out your differences with other people?" Talk this over and let them know that sometimes we have to take the first step in conflict resolution ourselves. Now ask: "What would it be like if people all over the world, including leaders of government, were committed first and foremost to working out differences nonviolently?"

If you find yourself reacting negatively right now, look to see if you have a vision of a peaceful world. Do you believe peace is possible? Take a moment to think about this now. Close your eyes and just picture what the world would be like if it were completely at peace. Imagine the details. Now stay with your vision and let it develop. What did you come up with? Could you envision a world at peace, or was something in the way? If so, what was it? Talk about this with others and invite them to engage in the process of envisioning a world at peace. The vision is the source as well as the goal. Taking steps to incorporate the skills of peacemaking into your life begins with a vision that peace is possible. The goal or destination is the realization of the vision. The whole process starts with you, as an individual. Reflect for a moment on the possibility that global peace may begin with you.

CLASS (OR FAMILY) MEETINGS:

There are different ways to create an atmosphere of peace in the school and home. The class or family meeting helps you to set the context for cooperation. If you set the tone through discussions, you'll find it easier to establish mutual agreements to solve problems. If possible, have a class or family meeting at least once a week at a set time. In the classroom, sitting in a circle on the floor or in chairs works best. This creates a sense of equal partnership—no one's in the front or back of the room—and also a feeling of connectedness. In the home, the best place to hold meetings is at the kitchen table. When young children are involved, the teacher or parent can run the meetings. Alternate this leadership role with older children.

Rules for meetings might be:

- The goal is to improve the atmosphere in the class or home, not to rehash differences or "dump."
- Each person gets a turn to speak.
- There are no interruptions.
- Each person must agree not to make negative comments about any other person.
- Each person must listen to the speaker.
- Each person must agree to consider things from the speaker's perspective rather than focusing only on his own thoughts.

Write down any group decisions or agreements—ones that are based upon full class or family discussion and participation—and post them where they can easily be seen. As the meeting goes along, the facilitator may want to thank each person who expresses an opinion or idea; this acknowledges participation and encourages those who might tend to be reticent.

Class or family meetings provide the opportunity for airing differences, resolving problems, and working together cooperatively. Children enjoy being included in the decision-making process — it helps them become more autonomous and responsible. Also, the sense of the class or family as a unit emerges out of this kind of participation.

DISCIPLINING WITH LOVE: SOME GUIDELINES

Utilize the following guidelines to enhance your ability to nurture peaceful behaviors:

1. *Remember that you are capable of reaching each child.* Studies prove that children from classes (families) in which their teachers (parents) believe in them and expect them to succeed, generally, do succeed. Where academic expectations are negative, negative performance follows. So it is with behavior. When you expect the negative, you get it. When you know that each child is capable of behaving and cooperating, and when you act on this belief, you evoke positive behaviors. You will drastically reduce the need for disciplinary measures by focusing on and expecting the positive.

2. *Catch children in the act of doing something right and acknowledge them immediately.*

This guideline doesn't mean ignoring negative behavior but rather shifting the focus from negative to positive attention. It works. Try it. You can also start by making a list of all the positive attributes of the child who is giving you the most difficulty. Share this list with the child to support his or her self-image. Each time you see that child engaged in a positive behavior, acknowledge him or her for it. You can add to the list daily as well. Keep doing this and see what happens.

Catching your students in the act of "doing it right:"

The class is noisy. You want the children to settle down for the next lesson. You state: "Boys and girls I'd like you to settle down, take out your math books, and show me you're ready to begin the lesson." The majority of the class continues to talk. Five children are following your direction. You state: "Kathy, I like the way you're taking out your math book and getting ready for the lesson. You're sitting quietly, too. Thanks. Eric, you're also following directions

really well. You're ready for the lesson. Your pencils and eraser are out and your book is already open to the correct page. That's great."

You will begin to notice that each time you sincerely acknowledge positive behaviors, others in the class will begin to follow. As this happens, give a brief acknowledgment to each child: "Terry, you're ready too. Great." And so on until the class has become quiet and attentive, at which time you can acknowledge them as a group. Children love to be noticed. If they can't draw your attention with positive behaviors, they'll try the opposite. Everyone wins when the focus is on the positive.

Catching your children in the act of "doing it right" at home:

Your children are playing a game. Two of them are arguing and annoying each other. The third is playing quietly, not participating in the argument. You might say: "Jess, I like the way you've been playing cooperatively. You're being considerate of your brothers. Thanks." Notice what the others do when you react this way: More than likely, they'll follow the positive lead when you acknowledge (affirm) the one acting positively. It's not necessary to call attention to the negative behaviors. Haim Ginott brilliantly describes this process in *Teacher & Child* [1] — a must read for anyone who wants to create a positive learning/living environment.

If the negative behaviors continue, you have several alternatives:

Give Choices: "Jason and Carl, you can either stop arguing or put the game away."

Make a Request: "I'd like to ask you to play quietly now. It disturbs me to see you arguing. Are you willing to stop arguing and continue your game?"

Time Out: "It seems to me that you boys need a break from one another. Jason you sit at the kitchen table for a while. Carl, you sit on the couch. When you feel ready to resume playing calmly you can return to the game."

Apply the Win/Win guidelines (see next chapter).

NOTE: I strongly urge you to pick up a copy of *Parent Effectiveness Training* by Thomas Gordon[2] or *Effectiveness Training for Women* (great for men, too) by Linda Adams[3]. These books provide excellent background on the use of effective listening tools and "I messages," which you will need if you have no such prior experience. Keep a copy of one or both of these references in your classroom or home.

Notice that none of the above techniques passes judgment or levies a punishment. This is not to say that punishment is never appropriate. When all else has failed, punishment may be the next step. Just remember, if you punish, avoid name calling, judging, or moralizing. Simply address the behavior you want changed and state your feeling about it.

Example:

"Now I'm angry, Jason and Carl. I've asked you to stop arguing and you've chosen to continue anyway. I'm losing my patience and I want you to go to your rooms."

Notice the difference between this interaction and the following:

(Name Calling): "Jason and Carl, you're a couple of pests and you're driving me crazy."

(Judging): "What a naughty thing to do! You deserve to be punished because you're being so bad."

(Moralizing): "If you were good boys you would stop fighting when I ask you to. When I was little I always listened to my mother."

The parent in the first example allowed her children to understand her position without making them feel attacked. When people feel attacked, they don't want to cooperate.

There is a form of creative punishment that you might wish to try called "conditional punishment," in which a privilege is revoked but the child is given the opportunity to earn it back through positive behavior.

Example:

"OK Jason and Carl. You've had the chance to work out your differences, but you're not cooperating. Tonight you won't be able to watch T.V. However, there is a way you can earn back the privilege. If you can play the game together without annoying one another,

I'll consider allowing you to earn back the privilege to watch one show this evening."

3. *Use reward systems.*

Make a chart. Write down behaviors you want the particular child to accomplish. Have the child meet with you each morning and at the end of the day to review the goals set out on the chart and the progress made. This can be done at school and/or at home.

The following format can be used:

Tim's Star Chart	Mon.	Tues.	Wed.	Thurs.	Fri.
I completed my class-work.					
I finished my homework.					
I got along with the children sitting next to me.					
I did neat and careful work.					
I paid attention in class.					

Each time the child accomplishes the indicated behavior, put a star on the chart. If you're doing this in school, at the end of each week write a note to the child's parents indicating how many goals were accomplished. Don't use the chart for negative reinforcement by stressing goals not accomplished. Praise the child for what he/she achieved, and be specific about it. For example, "Tim, you completed all your homework as well as your classwork today. Everything was neat and carefully done. Congratulations." This type of praise is much more effective than, "You did good work." After the child has been steadily accomplishing his or her goals, start to phase out the chart so it doesn't become a crutch.

4. *Express lots of love.*

The more you focus on loving feelings, the less room there will be for negative ones. Imagine yourself as a radio with lots of adjustable dials. You can "fine tune" your listening so your radio picks up that which is positive about a particular child. Keep noticing the good points. In fact, make that list of attributes we talked about before. Keep expanding the list each time you notice a new one. Share the list with the child, and let him/her feel acknowledged.

5. *Be kind to yourself.*

In today's busy society, we sometimes inflict a subtle form of violence upon ourselves called stress. This comes about through pressure, overwork, and excessive expectations. When you are tense and burdened, it's hard to act in a loving way. In his book, *One Minute for Myself,* Spencer Johnson suggests taking a minute several times a day and asking, "Is there a way for me to take better care of myself right now?"[4] Try it—you may begin to feel less pressured and thus more relaxed with others. In treating yourself lovingly, you spread the positive feeling to those around you. If you're a teacher, see if you and another teacher (or teachers) can support each other in being good to yourselves. Little things count—a walk together at lunchtime, a quiet moment together after school where you can let your hair down.

6. *Have fun together.*

As a teacher or parent, planning "fun" into your days is important. Light, relaxing, joyful, or silly activities can take the edge off a busy day. Five minutes of fun can spark energy and create a more alive atmosphere wherever you might be. Imagine laughter as the antidote to deprivation of the spirit. When we allow ourselves to experience the joy of human interconnectedness, our relationships flourish. Plan at least one fun activity each day, even if it is only for a few minutes. You will notice the difference this makes for you as well as the children.

Footnotes:
[1] Ginott, Haim, *Teacher & Child,* New York: MacMillan, 1972.
[2] Gordon, Thomas, *Parent Effectiveness Training,* New York: Peter Weyden, 1970.
[3] Adams, Linda, *Effectiveness Training for Women,* New York: Weyden Books, 1979.
[4] Johnson, Spencer, *One Minute for Myself,* New York: WeydenBooks, 1979.

THE WIN/WIN GUIDELINES: SHOWCASING CONFLICT RESOLUTION SKILLS

The Win/Win Guidelines for conflict resolution are critical to learning the skills of peacemaking. I present them below as well as in several lessons in this book. The Win/Win Guidelines are the basis for teaching the essential process of conflict resolution.

THE WIN/WIN GUIDELINES

1. Take time for cooling off, if needed. Find alternative ways to express anger.

2. Using "I messages," each person states his/her feelings and the problem as he/she sees it. No blaming, no name-calling, no interrupting.

3. Each person states the problem as the other person sees it.

4. Each person states how he/she is responsible for the problem.

5. Brainstorm solutions together and choose a solution that satisfies both—a Win/Win solution.

6. Affirm your partner.

Showcasing is especially helpful when teaching conflict resolution. Showcasing simply means that from time to time you work out individual conflicts with the entire class participating. The following is a condensed example of a sixth grade teacher's application of the Win/Win Guidelines during a social studies lesson. In this case, the class is already familiar with the process.

You are teaching a social studies lesson. Mandy and Sara are whispering to one another. Suddenly Sara tears up a piece of paper and throws it at Mandy. You stop the lesson.

Teacher: What's going on, girls?

Sara: She wrote something nasty on that paper about me.

Mandy: It wasn't nasty. I was just making a joke.

Sara: Some joke. It wasn't funny, and I think you're a creep.

Other students start whispering and calling out, "What did she say about you, Sara?"

Sara: Just shut up and leave me alone.

Teacher: Enough. Sara I know you're upset right now, and I'd like to help you and Mandy work this problem out the way we discussed, using the Win/Win Guidelines.

Sara: I don't want to work anything out with her. I hate her.

Teacher: I know you're angry at Mandy, but you're also friends. If you're willing I can help you work out this difference so you can continue to be friends. Remember, the alternative is that you'll both miss recess tomorrow. Which would you rather do?

Mandy: I guess the Win/Win Guidelines.

Sara: All right (pouting).

Teacher: Are you able to do it now, or do you need time to cool off? [They both agree to do it now.] I'd like to allow the class to be part of the process so we can *all* learn how to work out our differences. Is that OK with the two of you?

Mandy: Yes.

Sara: As long as no one makes fun of me.

Teacher: Class, do you agree not to make any put downs of any kind?

Class: Yes.

Teacher: Good. Let's begin. But I must stress something else first. There's no interrupting. If anyone interrupts, the process stops. (*Note:* This is *vital*, or the process can take all day and you will be drained.) Do you all agree? (Everyone nods.) So we'll start by stating the problem. Let me also remind you that whatever you say has to come from a *commitment to resolving the conflict.* OK?

Mandy & Sara: OK.

Teacher: Would you each describe the problem as you see it. Sara, you go first.

Sara: It's what I said before. She wrote something nasty about me.

Mandy: That's because she said my new shirt is ugly.

Sara: It is ugly.

Teacher: Sara, let me remind you of your commitment to working this out. Otherwise, I won't waste the class's time.

Sara: Sorry.

Mandy: I think the problem is that Sara put down what I was wearing. So I put her down to get even.

Teacher: It sounds like you both insulted each other. How did you feel, Mandy, when Sara insulted you?

Mandy: Real angry.

Teacher: How about you, Sara?

Sara: I wanted to hit her.

Teacher: I'm glad you didn't because problems aren't usually worked out by hitting. Sara, can you pretend you're Mandy just for a moment and state the problem as she sees it?

Sara: OK. Mandy felt put down by what I said about her shirt. She probably felt embarrassed, too, because I said it in front of the other kids.

Teacher: Thanks, Sara. How about you Mandy. Can you pretend you're Sara for a moment, and state the problem as she sees it?

Mandy: OK. Sara got angry because I wrote her a nasty note after she made fun of what I was wearing. Sometimes Sara does that when I ignore her and talk to Melissa.

Teacher: Sara, how are you responsible for the problem?

Sara: I made fun of Mandy's shirt.

Teacher: How are you responsible, Mandy?

Mandy: I wrote her a nasty note.

Teacher: What can the two of you do to avoid having this kind of confrontation again? I'd like you to come up with a lot of different ideas and the class can make suggestions, too. In the end, you two can decide what would be the best solution.

Sara: She can stop calling me names.

Mandy: Sara can stop making fun of the clothes I wear. I can't help it if she has nicer clothes.

Student: Mandy and Sara can trade clothes sometimes.

Student: Mandy and Sara can go shopping together.

Student: Mandy can include Sara when Melissa's around so she doesn't feel ignored.

Sara: Mandy and I can be more considerate of each other's feelings and stop using put downs.

Mandy: I can tell Sara when I'm angry with her instead of calling her a name.

Student: You can write each other notes to explain why you're mad at each other instead of using them to insult each other.

Teacher: Sounds like we've got lots of good ideas. Girls, what solution do you want to choose?

Sara: How about if we're more considerate of each other's feelings?

Mandy: Yeah. And we can also just tell each other when we're angry instead of calling names.

Teacher: Thanks girls. I'm pleased with the way you worked this out. Could you affirm each other?

Sara: Thanks Mandy and I'm sorry I got so mad.

Mandy: It's OK. I'm sorry too and I'm glad we're still friends.

This process takes about ten minutes and is a valuable group exercise in conflict resolution. Showcasing doesn't need to be done very often, but it's particularly helpful when the class is just beginning to learn the Win/Win Guidelines. The class gets to participate in the process and sees the outcome. It also serves as a model for future cooperative behavior and problem solving.

As your students integrate and apply the conflict resolution process, they will need you less and less as a mediator. Eventually, they will be able to apply the guidelines without you. They do not have to do every step every time, either. Remember that the ten minutes you take out of your lessons to occasionally showcase conflict resolution skills will pay off over and over again as your students become more cooperative and able to work out their differences. Once that happens, you can send the "adversaries" off to an area of the room where they can work out their problem.

READY, SET, GO

Now you're ready to go. Don't forget to skim through the book before you begin, and please adapt these lessons to your particular classroom or family situation. Dialogue has been included within each lesson to make your job easier, but don't be confined by it. Change the words to fit your style, and bring the richness of your own experiences into each lesson.

As you do each lesson, you might consider sharing personal anecdotes during circle discussion. For example, in Lesson 1 you'll be discussing visions of a peaceful classroom. Share yours first. It will help the children to open up. They'll also appreciate hearing about your feelings and ideas.

Another thing to stress—good listening. As each child speaks, ask every other student in the class to focus on him/her. Ask each child to look *directly* at the speaker. Begin to have each child ask the rest of the class to look at him/her when he/she speaks. For example, Shawna is going to

share. She looks around the circle and sees other children talking. She says, "Class could you please look at me, I'd like to share something." Don't let her begin to share until every eye is on her and every ear is atuned.

I'd love to hear how the program works for you. If you have additional lesson ideas that correspond to the understandings in this book, please write and tell me about them. You can reach me by writing to the following address:

Naomi Drew
32 First Avenue
Spotswood, New Jersey 08884

Now, bring the lessons to your students with my best wishes and with deep hope that their futures and yours will be happy, loving, and peaceful.

STAGE I:
PEACE BEGINS WITH ME

"...I speak of a futuristic ideal which exalts wisdom, sensitivity, fairness, and compassion as basic requirements in running the affairs of the world. A new world, the world I long for, cannot be built with the tools, psychology, or belief system of old. It will be born of the changes encoded in the details of our lives as we are living them now. The fabric of the new society will be made of nothing more or less than the threads woven in today's interactions."

Pam McAllister,
Reweaving the Web of Life

CREATING A PEACEFUL CLASSROOM

OBJECTIVES

- The teacher and students will create the setting for a peaceful classroom.
- The students will list qualities of a peaceful classroom.

MATERIALS

- Two large pieces of chart paper
- Markers
- Copies of the Parent letter (see Page 21)
- "Friends" (see Page 22)

PROCEDURE

1. Create within yourself an image of every child in your class as whole, perfect, and capable. Picture yourself speaking to your class out of this image. Focus on the promise of each child and imagine this year being the realization of this promise. Also, envision the promise of you as teacher, impacting your students for the rest of their lives out of the way you interact with them this year. Picture your students as responsible, productive, and caring individuals. Know that you have the ability to help them develop in this way. Now you are ready to have a dialogue with your students.

2. Ask students to sit in a circle either on the floor or in chairs. The circle connects them visually and allows them to see each other. It is helpful to have a permanent space in the room where you can easily form a circle.

3. Say, "Out of my care for you, I want to find new ways to have a peaceful future. We often hear about people hurting each other or not caring about one another. I started to picture what the world would be like if teachers everywhere began to teach their students how to get along and accept other people. What kind of world would it be? Peace starts with each individual, and the way you act affects the world around you." Allow the children to respond.

4. Express your interest in getting to know each student and your willingness to be there for them if they have a problem. You might say something like, "I want us to have a great year together. Out of our cooperation and care for

one another we can all help to make this happen."

5. Speak about the need for everyone in the class to work as partners, to cooperate, and to be considerate. Discuss the meaning of the word "considerate." Stress the need for each member to take responsibility for having a peaceful atmosphere in the class. Ask, "What does taking responsibility mean to you?" Discuss.

6. Ask, "How do you want it to be in our room throughout the year? How do you want to be treated and how do you want to treat others?" You can begin by stating some of the ways you would like the class to be. (Example: I want the children to be considerate of one another.)

7. After the children have discussed the kind of class atmosphere they want, you can label this atmosphere as "peaceful." On a piece of chart paper write: A Peaceful Classroom Is One in Which . . .

8. Ask your students to reiterate the qualities of a peaceful classroom on the chart. It may start something like this: "A peaceful classroom is one in which . . . We are considerate of each other. We speak quietly. We pay attention when someone else is speaking. We don't call each other names." You can keep expanding this chart throughout the year.

9. After you complete the chart together, ask the children what a "nonpeaceful" classroom might be like? Discuss. Ask what it would take, on the part of each student, to have the class be

the way they want it to be. Discuss.

10. Ask your students if they will all agree to do whatever it takes to create a peaceful classroom and bring to life what they listed on the chart. Tell them that the chart can serve as a guide to follow during the year, and that additions can be made to it at any time.

11. Ask if anyone feels that they might have a problem abiding by the "rules" on the chart. Discuss. Stress the need for cooperation and the fact that everyone working together will make a huge difference.

12. Ask the class to sign an agreement which states, "We agree to follow the rules we created together to have a peaceful classroom." Hang this next to "A Peaceful Classroom Is One in Which . . ." chart.

13. Copy the Peaceful Classroom chart and send it home to your students' parents with a note (suggested wording on Page 21).

14. Discuss the note with your class. Ask them to discuss it and the chart rules with their families for homework.

15. Conclude by reading Friends (see Page 22).

Lesson 1
Learning the Skills of Peacemaking

Dear Parent(s),

Our class has developed a set of rules (attached) which we have all agreed to follow throughout the year. We invite you to be our partners in the goal of having a peaceful classroom this year. Would you save these rules and talk them over with me?

Throughout the year we'll be doing other activities like this from a program called Learning the Skills of Peacemaking. In this program we are learning that peace starts with each individual, and that it's important for all of us to take responsibility for our actions.

If you have any questions about the program, or our rules for a peaceful classroom, my teacher would be happy to speak to you.

Thanks very much.

Child's Name

FRIENDS
Words and Music by Jonathan Sprout

Have you ever travelled far away to another town?
Did you feel like a stranger when you were there?
It's just a state of mind. You can feel at home anywhere.
Anywhere you go, there are kids who care.
There are no towns full of bad people.
In every town there are good people.
And just like you and me
They wish we all were friends.
Far away in countries all around the world
There are millions of people we may never see.
But they're reaching out and they're opening up their hearts.
And they want to be friends with you and me.
There are no countries full of bad people.
In every country there are good people.
And just like you and me
They wish that we were friends.
Everywhere you look today
People want to give.
It doesn't matter what they say,
We all should live
As friends!
No matter where we live
Or what language we speak
No matter what religion we believe in
No matter how we dress
Or what lifestyle we seek
No matter the color of our skin.

I'M A SPECIAL AND UNIQUE PERSON

OBJECTIVES

- The children will complete "Me Mobiles" with the headings:

    1. Me

    2. My best friend

    3. My family

    4. My favorite food

    5. My favorite color

    NOTE: The teacher can write the headings ahead of time, or the children can do this when they receive their mobile papers.

- The children will learn to use the Guidelines for Sharing.

- The children will experience an increased sense of self-esteem through awareness and sharing.

- The children will understand that the statement "Peace begins with me" means, in part, feeling good about themselves.

MATERIALS

- "I Am An Individual" chart (see Page 25 — you can make one for each child if you wish)

- Five 5 x 7 square pieces of construction paper per child for "Me Mobile" sections (see illustration on Page 26)

- Hangers, yarn, scissors, hole punchers

- Crayons, markers

- Chart

GUIDELINES FOR SHARING

Everybody gets a chance to speak.

Each person listens while others are speaking.

Focus on the speaker, not your own thoughts.

Everyone waits their turn.

Don't say or do anything to put one another down.

Don't interrupt.

PROCEDURE

1. Have the children sit in a circle on the floor cross-legged.

2. Read "I Am An Individual." Explain anything the children don't understand. Discuss. Reiterate the fact that we are all special and unique. Tell the children that they will be doing a project which will focus on their specialness. Tell the children they will first learn a way to create calmness in their classroom and in their lives. Ask them to sit very still with their eyes closed. Say, "Picture your mind as a blank movie screen. Nothing is present. You are looking at the blank screen. Now picture on your screen the ocean, calm and quiet. No one is there, not even you, just the ocean, sky, sand, air, and maybe a passing gull. Picture the waves gently breaking on the shore. Picture the sun reflecting off each wave. Feel a gentle wind move by." You can continue quietly describing this scene in your own words for a moment or two. The whole process should last about three minutes. When everyone is perfectly still say, "Listen to the quiet. Feel the calmness we have created. Now gently open your eyes."

3. Say, "We will be recreating this calmness often throughout the school year. The calmness helps you feel good inside. It also helps you think and learn."

NOTE: This technique is invaluable. It can be used at the start of each day or at the start of different lessons. It can also be used at times when your class is noisy. You can stop everything for several minutes, do this technique, and then resume teaching in a more relaxed atmosphere.

4. Say, "What is the most special thing about you? Is it something you can do like ride a bike (adapt this for older children), or the color of your hair, or a certain way you are, like kind or generous. Think about this, and we'll go around the circle and tell each other what's the most special thing about us."

5. Refer to the Guidelines for Sharing. Say, "As we take our turns, these guidelines will help us listen and speak as a group. Discuss each guideline and make sure it's understood.

6. Begin the circle discussion by saying, "The most special thing about me is." Encourage each child to share. Other children can help those who are shy or embarrassed by saying things like, "I think Janie is special because she's always nice to other people." Children who feel awkward can "pass" but should be encouraged to raise their hands later if they think of something to share.

7. Proceed around the circle. Encourage each child to finish the sentence, "The most special thing about me is. . ."

8. Pass out the "Me Mobile" parts. Read and describe each heading referred to in the objectives. Write these headings on the board for the children to copy in small letters. Have the children draw an illustration for each heading.

9. Children should be encouraged to talk quietly with their neighbors about what they are drawing. This can be done at their seats, in the circle, or in small groups.

10. Display the completed mobiles in the classroom or in the halls. Discuss the mobiles together and continue to stress the specialness and uniqueness of each child. Say, "We all have a contribution to make to the world around us as the result of our specialness." Discuss the meaning of the word contribution.

11. As a follow-up game, you can ask the children to form groups according to "favorites." For example ask everyone whose favorite food is pizza to go to the back of the room. Then the children introduce themselves to one another. Or, have half the class pick names out of a box containing papers with names of the other half of the class in it. The children find their partners. Then they read and discuss each other's "Me Mobiles" and compare "favorites."

NOTE: Younger children (grade 1) may have some difficulty drawing the details of their favorite things early in the year, so this activity can be saved for a later time when small muscle coordination is better developed. Instead, young children can draw a large picture of "My Family and Me." Favorite things can be spoken about and listed on a chart, or a large collage can be made of "favorites" cut out from magazines. However, with older students (grades 2-6) this is an excellent activity for the first week of school.

I AM AN INDIVIDUAL

by Naomi Drew

I am an individual.
I have dignity and worth.
I am unique.
I deserve respect and I respect others.
I am part of the human family.
I have something special to offer the world.
I am committed to a peaceful world for all of us.
I make a difference, and so do you.
I can accomplish whatever I set out to do, and so can you.
I am the key to peace.

"ME" MOBILE

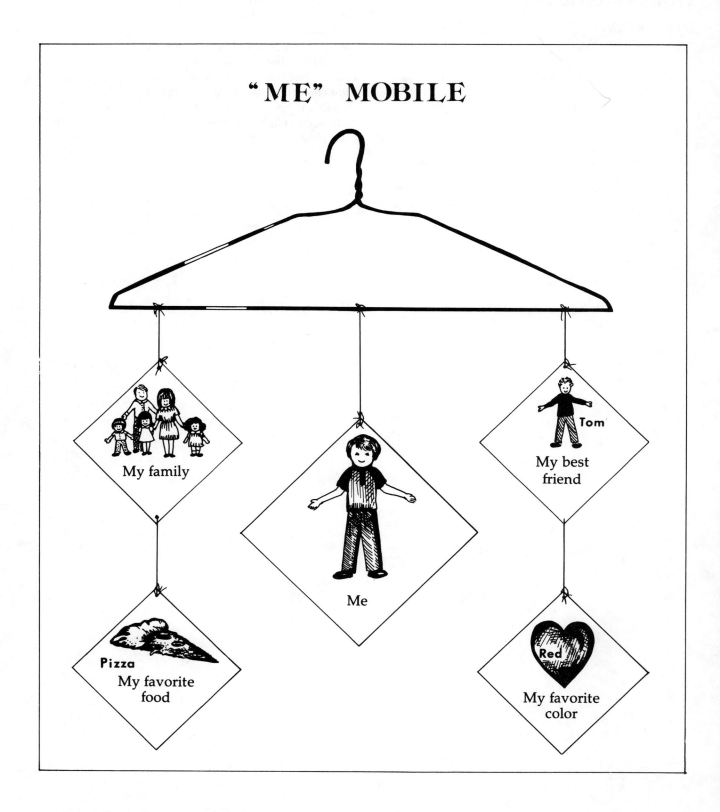

DEFINING PEACE

OBJECTIVES

- The children will explore personal meanings of peace.

- The children will learn one definition of peace: "Peace means taking care of ourselves, each other, and our earth."

- The children will learn that peace is personal but also denotes a sense of responsibility and a commitment to others and the environment.

MATERIALS

- Guidelines for Sharing

- Large paper with words written on it in bright letters: "What Peace Feels Like to Me"

- "Peace means taking care of ourselves, each other, and our earth" on a poster

- Posters or pictures from magazines showing the following:

    a. People taking care of themselves (emotional and physical well-being)

    b. People taking care of each other (love, assistance)

    c. People taking care of the earth (environment)

    Children can bring these in ahead of time.

- Posters or pictures showing the result of people not taking care of themselves, one another, the earth. Children can bring these in ahead of time.

- Drawing paper and crayons for young children. Writing paper and pencils (for older children)

    NOTE: This lesson correlates with Bulletin Board 1, entitled "Peace Means Taking Care of Ourselves, Each Other, and Our Earth."

PROCEDURE

1. Have the children sit in a circle. Go over the Guidelines for Sharing.

2. Say, "In order to create a calm and peaceful atmosphere in our classroom, we are first going to close our eyes for a moment, and get very still. Let your body relax. Let a warm, calm, peaceful feeling flow through every part of you from the tips of the toes to the top of your head. Listen to your own breathing. Listen to the perfect silence and calmness in our room. Now take a moment and think about what peace feels like to you." Give students a moment of silence in which to do this.

3. Ask your students to open their eyes. Say, "What does peace feel like to you?" On the large paper entitled "What Peace Feels Like to Me," record their answers. Accept anything, but try to guide your students away from the stereotyped concepts of peace. This exercise allows students to explore their beliefs and feelings about peace.

4. Ask, "What does peace look like to you? How does this room look when it's peaceful? How does your home and the people in it look when they are peaceful? How does your street or neighborhood look when it is peaceful? How do you think our earth would look if it were peaceful?" Discuss. Encourage lots of participation. Acknowledge each child's response. Continue to guide your children away from the stereotyped meanings of peace. Allow them to draw from their own experiences of peacefulness.

5. Say, "Here is one definition of peace: 'Peace means taking care of ourselves, each other, and our earth.'" Show the sign you have made with these words on it. Be sure this is written in large, bright letters. This will serve as a sign to be displayed in the room.

6. Ask a child to read the sign aloud. Discuss.

7. Show pictures of people taking care of themselves, etc. Have the students describe what they see in the pictures. Ask, "Why is taking care of ourselves important if we want peace?" Stress this: Peace starts with the individual. Tell the students that when they take care of themselves, they are meeting their physical, emotional, and safety needs. Ask, "How do you feel when your needs are not met?" Guide students to see that when their needs are not met, they do not feel peaceful inside.

8. Show pictures depicting results of not taking care of themselves, each other, and the earth. Have students describe and discuss. Encourage full participation.

9. Ask students to draw or write about a time when they have taken care of themselves, someone else, or the environment. Have them share their pictures and stories. Allow time for discussion. Thank each child who shares.

10. Ask, "Where does peace start?" Guide the children to reiterate that peace starts with the individual. Have the children work in small groups, each child writing or drawing his or her own definition or idea of peace. Explain that the way they work together can be a peacemaking activity. Ask, "How can we be peaceful as we work together?" Encourage the sharing of ideas.

11. Have the children read or show their definitions or pictures of what they interpret peace to be. Discuss. Hang the pictures on the bulletin board, and enjoy them. Each time you need some extra peacefulness inside, look at the pictures.

Bulletin Board 1
Learning the Skills of Peacemaking

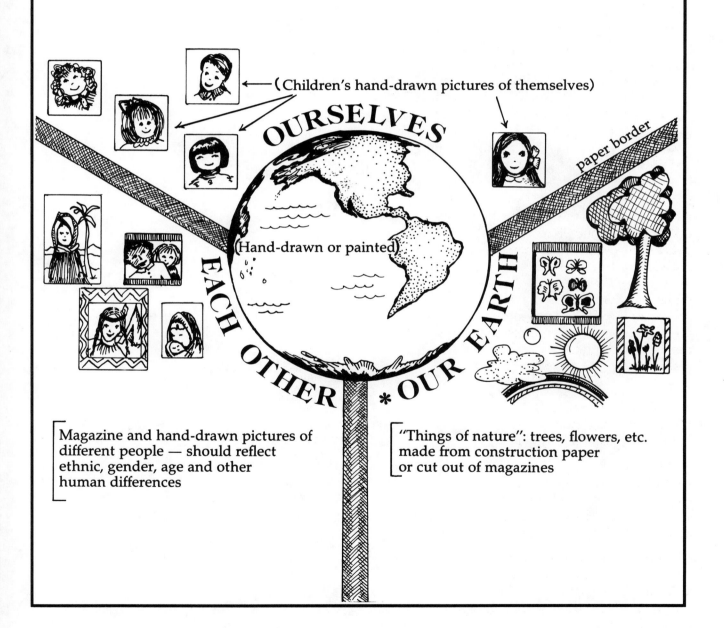

PEACE MEANS TAKING CARE OF OURSELVES, EACH OTHER, & OUR EARTH

←(Children's hand-drawn pictures of themselves)

OURSELVES

paper border

(Hand-drawn or painted)

EACH OTHER

*OUR EARTH

Magazine and hand-drawn pictures of different people — should reflect ethnic, gender, age and other human differences

"Things of nature": trees, flowers, etc. made from construction paper or cut out of magazines

THE PROCESS OF AFFIRMING

OBJECTIVES

- The children will understand that peace starts with the individual, and when they affirm others they create an atmosphere of acceptance that is crucial to peacemaking.

- The children will understand and use the process of affirmation in school and at home.

MATERIALS

- Poem: "Being Human is Being Special"
- "The Process of Affirming" Poster:

THE PROCESS OF AFFIRMING

First, just notice what is special about the other person.

Make a sincere statement to the other person about whatever is positive or special about him/her.

Be sure to look at the other person directly as you speak.

Relax, and know that the other person is just like you inside.

- Paper and pencils for kids old enough to express themselves through writing; crayons and drawing paper for younger children

PROCEDURE

1. Ask the class to sit in a circle.

2. Read the poem "Being Human Is Being Special" (see Page 33).

3. State, "Each of you is very special. I like being your teacher. I think you're great." Pause and look at your students. Ask them how they felt when you just spoke the words you did. Tell them that what you just did was to affirm them. Say, "When we affirm, we make a sincere, positive statement about another person or people."

4. Ask, "How do you feel when people affirm you?" Discuss. Don't be surprised if some students express feelings of embarrassment and awkwardness at being acknowledged. This is natural.

5. Refer to the poster: The Process of Affirming. Read it to the class. Remind the class that

peace begins with each of us. When we affirm one another it creates an atmosphere of acceptance that is crucial to peacemaking. Say, "When we feel accepted by other people it becomes easier to work out our differences with them. We're all the same inside, but sometimes we forget that. Affirming helps connect us in a special way. Today we're going to learn to affirm one another. We can affirm people any time at all. The more we concentrate on the positive things about people, the easier it is to get along."

6. State, "Now we're going to have the opportunity to affirm one another in pairs. This is especially important if your partner is someone you don't usually 'hang around' with. Remember that not having peace often results from not accepting people who are different from us in some way. Boys and girls not accepting one another is a perfect example of

this. How many boys in here have felt negatively toward another person because that person happens to be a girl? Ask for a show of hands. "How many girls have had negative feelings toward others because those people happen to be boys?" Ask for a show of hands.

7. Say, "Peace starts with the individual and it starts with the daily decisions we make about other people. If we're committed to being peacemakers, then we must decide to focus more on likenesses than differences. We need to remember our commitment to peace even when we are faced with barriers." Explain the meaning of barriers.

8. Say, "Now you will have an opportunity to overcome a barrier, to be a peacemaker, and to affirm someone else — even if that person isn't someone you normally play with."

9. Say, "Turn and face the person who is sitting next to you. Each person should have a partner. Acknowledge that person by nodding your head. Remember that any negative faces or comments you might make are a put-down to that person. Be kind."

10. Say, "Now, close your eyes and get very calm and relaxed. Let any negative thoughts leave you. If they come back just let them pass. In a moment I will ask you to open your eyes and look into the eyes of your partner, very calmly without speaking. Open your eyes now. Just look at the person you're sitting across from. Notice that this person has eyes, nose, mouth and hair — just like you. Realize that this person has a brain and a heart beating inside—just like you. Know that this person has the same need for love and acceptance that you have. Take a good look at one another. Now close your eyes again. Picture the other person in your mind. Recall his or her facial features and hair color. Try to think of how your partner feels right now. Open your eyes and look at your partner again."

11. Say, "Now close your eyes one more time and think of something positive about your partner. Is it his or her smile, or eyes, or is it something about the way this person acts that's positive? Now open your eyes and affirm your partner, stating the positive quality you thought of." Allow time for the partners to

affirm one another. Some might need coaching from the teacher. Every student should be encouraged to complete the affirmation.

12. Have the students face front in a circle. Ask, "How did you feel during this activity?" Discuss. Allow the feelings of awkwardness to surface, especially in older children. Encourage their honesty and candor. Affirm them for participating.

13. Now state, "I am going to affirm each of you." Go around the circle and say something positive to each child. Be careful to notice your own barriers. If you're comfortable, shake hands, or put your hand on an arm or shoulder as you speak.

> NOTE: When I did this with my class, I held both hands as I spoke to each child. It was very moving; in fact, I had to blink back tears as I looked deeply into the eyes of each of my students. A strong feeling of warmth and care connected us. It was a special moment that brought us all closer together.

14. If there's time, repeat the process with the same partners. Say, "Let's affirm our partners again." Restate the importance of affirming others. Ask the students to affirm someone when they go home.

15. Ask each student to draw an "affirmation picture" of their partner. This picture should reflect the positive quality they noticed in that person. Below the picture, older children can write the affirmation too. Example: "Billy is kind. He shares his eraser with me."

> NOTE: Depending on your class and the age of your students, you can expand affirmations to include handshaking and hugs. In my class, it eventually became very normal to see children hug one another. A wonderful experience arose out of a conflict between two of my "tough" little boys. One child asked me to mediate a conflict. I asked if he would go back to the child with whom he was having the conflict, work it out, and then affirm one another. In time I noticed the two boys talking, then shaking hands, and eventually hugging.

BEING HUMAN IS BEING SPECIAL

by Naomi Drew

I look in the mirror and who do I see.
My very own person who looks just like me.
I look at my eyes, I look at my face,
Knowing that no one on earth or in space
Is quite like I am, one of a kind.
My body is special and so is my mind.
Each person alive has something special to give.
We each make a difference each day that we live.
I love myself and I love others too.
The world is a special place,
'Cause it has me and you.

DEFINING CONFLICT RESOLUTION

OBJECTIVES

- The children will understand one definition of conflict resolution.

- The children will understand and describe a conflict they have experienced in the classroom, with peers, or outside.

- The children will envision a solution to their conflict.

MATERIALS

- Chart for teacher to record children's responses entitled: Conflict Words/Conflict Resolution Words

PROCEDURE

1. Ask the children to form a discussion circle, and ask, "What is a conflict?" Discuss.

2. Say, "A conflict is a fight, a disagreement, or a problem. It usually involves more than one person. Often people become angry during a conflict. Conflict resolution is solving the problem so no one loses, and so that physical force is not used. When we resolve a conflict successfully, both sides feel like their needs have been met."

3. Say, "Today I want you to think of a specific conflict you have had that you weren't able to work out."

4. Allow the children briefly to share their conflicts aloud. Go around the circle and ask each child to make a statement. Example: "My friend and I had a fight over which game we should play during recess." Caution the children not to discuss anything too personal or to use names. Encourage each child in the room to share, stressing that conflict is a natural part of relationships. State, "We all have conflicts at one time or another. Anger is a natural feeling. There are ways of expressing our anger that work and there are ways that don't work." Explain "not working" as things we do which end up making matters worse, or don't help to resolve the conflict. Say, "Today we'll be thinking about ways that 'work.' In describing our conflict, think about how you 'worked things out' with the other person or if you

worked them out at all. Solutions that work satisfy both sides. These solutions are called 'Win/Win.'"

5. Say, "In order for a conflict to be resolved, at least one person needs to be committed to finding a solution that works." Ask the children to think of a time they worked something out with another person when both people felt satisfied in the end. Discuss.

6. Give a personal example.

7. Ask, "Have you ever worked out a conflict with someone who wasn't committed to working it out? Do you think it's possible to resolve a conflict when you are the only one committed to doing so? Give a personal example of a conflict you worked out, even when the other person wasn't committed."

8. Have the children sit in a circle. Say, "We're going to relax and think of a time we had a conflict. Close your eyes and allow a warm, relaxed feeling to come over you." Say, "In a little while, the warmth will flow into your brain and help you create a solution to the conflict you are thinking of. But first, think about that conflict a little more. Think of the words you spoke and the feelings you had when you were angry. Think of the words the other person spoke. Now think of a better way the conflict could have been resolved. Let that warm feeling help you picture a solution. Picture what you and the other person are

saying to solve the problem. Picture how your bodies are moving, your facial expressions and the room you are in. Picture yourselves working out the problem. Look at the other person's face. Now, look at your own. Try to feel the other person's feelings. Try to imagine what it's like to be that person. What words are you speaking to bring about your solution? Picture yourself happy and satisfied. Now open your eyes."

9. Have the children discuss the conflicts and solutions they pictured.

10. Ask the children to return to their seats. Pass out paper and have the children write "My Conflict" on one side, and "My Solution" on the other. Have them illustrate their conflict and solutions. They can write descriptions also.

11. After the children have drawn, or written, ask them to describe the pictures they have drawn of their conflicts and perceived solutions. Ask them to recall their images and state what they said in the conflict situation and in the solution of it.

12. As each child gives an example, ask, "In your image what did you say when you were angry? What did you say when you were solving the problem?" Record key phrases on the chart you have prepared entitled, "Conflict Words/Conflict Resolution Words." Example:

13. Guide the children to notice the distinction between the conflict words and the conflict resolution words. Help them to see that conflict words express anger and judgement. They close doors to communication. Conflict phrases often start with the word "you." On the other hand, conflict resolution words often denote compromise and conciliation. They open the doors. Often people ask questions and look for solutions when they use conflict resolution words.

14. Tell the children that it's hard for people to resolve conflicts when they are angry. Sometimes we need time to cool off first. Say, "In another lesson we're going to learn a set of guidelines which will help us resolve conflicts so each person wins. We'll talk about other conflicts we have had and ways we can solve them."

15. Say, "Take your papers home and share them with your families. Tell them what you discovered today about conflicts and solutions to them."

CONFLICT WORDS

(Example:)

"You'd better give me back my book right now!"

CONFLICT RESOLUTION WORDS

(Example:)

"Let's share the book until you find yours."

WHAT GETS IN THE WAY OF RESOLVING CONFLICTS

OBJECTIVES

- The children will reiterate the meaning of conflict and conflict resolution.

- The children will understand how they usually handle conflicts.

- The children will understand what emotions and thoughts impair their ability or willingness to resolve conflicts peacefully.

- The children will understand that they have choices in the way they resolve conflicts.

MATERIALS

- Story, "Michael's Bad Morning" (see below)

- Chalkboard, chalk

- Chart: Conflict Words/Conflict Resolution Words from Lesson 5

PROCEDURE

1. Have the children sit in a circle.

2. Tell them that they're going to hear a short story about a boy named Michael who has a fight at the bus stop. Say, "As you listen to the story, think about what caused the conflict, and how Michael felt."

3. Read: "Michael's Bad Morning."

MICHAEL'S BAD MORNING
It was Monday morning. Michael didn't want to get up and go to school. His bed felt so warm and inviting and it was cold outside. He opened his eyes slowly and noticed his dog, Prowler, lying on the floor chewing his brand new sneaker. "Prowler, get out of here!" he yelled angrily. Prowler ran off and hid in a corner.

He rose, slowly dressed, brushed his teeth and went downstairs, doubly angry because one of his new sneakers was ruined, plus he had to go to school today. "Why couldn't it still be Sunday?" he thought.

Michael ate breakfast, got his book bag, and went to the bus stop. The kids were playing kickball. As he bent over to put his bookbag down, the ball flew over and popped him in the head. "Ouch!" he yelled. "Who did that?"

It was Tommy who guiltily called out, "I didn't mean it, really," as the other kids laughed. Michael exploded.

"Oh yes you did, you dummy. See if you like the way it feels!" And with that, he lifted the ball and threw it back at Tommy, hitting him in the stomach.

Tommy yelled out, "Hey, that's not fair. The ball hit you by accident, but you did that on purpose. You're mean." This time Tommy threw the ball hard at Michael's leg. Next, the two boys were fighting.

4. Ask, "What caused the fight?" Discuss. Encourage the children to air their reactions.

5. Ask, "How would you have handled the situation if you were Michael, at the moment the ball hit you in the head?" Discuss.

6. Ask, "What got in the way of working out the problem?"

7. Ask, "Do you ever feel so angry you don't want to work out a problem?" Discuss and ask for examples. You can give your own personal example.

8. Ask, "What are some of the other choices Michael had, rather than throwing the ball back at Tommy?" Discuss, and list the children's

responses on the board under the heading "Other Choices." Some might be:

- Yell, but don't hurt the other person.
  Walk away until you've calmed down and then tell the person how you felt.

- Throw the ball hard in another direction so it doesn't hurt anyone.

- See the humor in the situation.
  Allow the responses to come from the children, but guide them to see that there are choices. Encourage them to come up with as many as possible.

9. Say, "Think of a time when you were angry and you didn't want to work it out. Turn to the person you are sitting next to and tell him or her about it. Take turns." Have the children share for several minutes.

10. Ask, "Who would like to tell the class about a conflict you have had that you didn't want to work out?" As each child shares, ask the question, "What got in the way of working it out?"

11. Ask, "What other choices did you have that you might not have been aware of?" Have the children turn to their partners and discuss. Next have them share as a group.

12. Say, "Even though you generally have choices in the way you handle conflicts, sometimes you might not be aware of those choices because you're too angry or upset. That's part of being human, and it doesn't mean you're bad. The thing to remember is to stop and think each time you have a conflict, and see if there's a different way you might handle it, so that in the end, the problem isn't worse." Discuss.

13. Say, "In the next lesson, you're going to learn about 'I messages' which will help you work out conflicts."

USING "I MESSAGES"

NOTE: Refer to *Parent Effectiveness Training,* by Thomas Gordon, or *Effectiveness Training for Women* by Linda Evans before doing this lesson. Giving "I Messages" is a complex communication technique. These books will help.

OBJECTIVES

- The children will role play problems that lead to conflict.

- The children will learn to use "I Messages" in conflict situations.

MATERIALS

- "I Messages/You Messages" poster

I MESSAGES

I feel angry.

I'm sad because you took my toy.

I'm embarrassed because you called me a name.

YOU MESSAGES

You're a pain.

You're mean.

You make me mad.

PROCEDURE

1. Have the children sit in a circle. Say, "Today we're going to do a fun relaxation exercise to start our lesson." Say, "Close your eyes and picture a great big scoop of your favorite ice cream. Put it on top of your favorite cone — sugar or wafer. Now put another scoop on top. Take a lick. Feel the cold smoothness of it on your tongue. Swallow the ice cream. Feel it going down your throat and into your stomach. Feel the coldness. Now take another lick and then a big bite. Feel the coldness on your teeth. Now, eat the whole thing. You're full now, rub your stomach and smile."

2. Say, "Now that you're all full, we're going to talk about something you can do when you have a conflict which will help you work out your differences."

3. Say, "What we're going to talk about is called 'I Messages.' There are two ways people can speak when they are talking about their feelings. People can start with either the word 'I' or 'You.'"

4. Say, "When you start with the word 'I' you don't place blame on others. 'I Messages' show that you are responsible for the way you feel. When you start with the word 'I' you don't put the other person on the defensive." Explain. Say "Remember, we all are responsible for our own feelings." Discuss.

5. Ask the students to look at the chart with "I/You Messages." Have a student read it aloud. Explain that "You Messages" put other people on the defensive and make them less likely to want to solve conflicts.

6. Set up some imaginary conflict situations.

Have students first use "You Messages," then "I Messages." Ask which worked better. Discuss. Encourage full participation. Thank the children who participate.

7. Students will role play the following situations, first as they would normally handle it, then using "I Messages."

> a. There is a pencil on the floor. Two people go to pick it up at once. They start to argue over whose pencil it is.

> b. Tom and Jason are walking to lunch. Mike asks if he can join them. Tom and Jason ignore Mike. Mike feels hurt.

> c. Maria and Peggy are working on a project together. Peggy hasn't brought the materials she is responsible for. Now the project might have to be turned in late.

> d. Alan's friend yelled at him this morning on the playground. Alan comes to school sad and upset. When another friend, Dave, says hello to him in line, Alan says "Get out of here!"
> After each role play, discuss what worked better, the "old way" or using "I Messages."

> NOTE: Giving "I Messages" is tricky. You might need to have your students practice it a few times before they get the hang of it.

8. Come up with other situations where the children can practice using "I Messages." Give them time to practice.

9. Ask, "How do you suppose this could work with countries who don't get along?"

10. Ask, "Do you think it's possible for nations to work out their differences through talking to one another?"

11. Ask, "Do you think it's worth the extra effort for nations to try this? Why?"

WIN/WIN GUIDELINES

OBJECTIVES

- The children will state the definitions of conflict and conflict resolution.

- The children will understand that conflict is a normal occurrence in relationships.

- The children will learn the Win/Win Guidelines as a way to solve conflicts peacefully.

- The children will playact conflict resolutions applying the Win/Win Guidelines.

MATERIALS

- Copies of Win/Win Guidelines for the students to take home

- Chart displaying the Win/Win Guidelines (see page 43)

PROCEDURE

1. State, "We have talked about conflicts we've had with people in our lives. Is it okay to have conflicts? Do all people have conflicts at one time or another?" Ask, "Is it possible to solve conflicts without hurting each other through our words or actions? When both people feel good at the end of a conflict, that is called Win/Win."

2. Say, "Today we are going to learn some guidelines that will help us deal with conflicts in such a way that both partners feel good, and so that no one loses."

3. Show the Win/Win Guidelines on the chart. It works well to have each guideline in a different color. Ask several students to read one guideline at a time.

4. Discuss each guideline. Ask what each guideline means to the students. Ask if they have ever tried to use any of these before. Ask if it worked. Discuss.

5. Discuss the word commitment. Remind students that a commitment is a promise one makes to oneself or someone else that is kept no matter what. Say, "Often we don't keep our promises when we are challenged too much. Commitment means that you keep your promise, regardless." State, "When at least one party in a conflict is committed to working the

problem out, then it is possible to use the Win/Win Guidelines successfully."

6. Ask, "If you have had a conflict with another person, and you're both angry, and then that other person calls you a name, should you stop being committed to working it out?" "What if the other person isn't committed to working it out? Should you decide not to be committed, too?" Discuss.

7. Ask, "Who does peace start with? Why is it important to keep your commitments?" Stress that there are times when it is difficult to be a peacemaker. Sometimes it is lonely to be the only one willing to work it out. Ask, "If we want to have a peaceful world, is it worth facing difficulties and sometimes working out the problem even if it's hard to do?" Discuss. Stress that peace starts with the commitment of individuals. Mention committed peacemakers like Martin Luther King, Corazon Aquino, Rosa Parks, and Gandhi who stood up for their beliefs even when they had little support.

8. Ask, "How do you think the countries of the world would get along if they were committed to working things out peacefully?"

NOTE: The next step should be repeated at least once a week throughout the year. Also, don't forget to use the Win/Win

Guidelines to "showcase," as described in the chapter "The Win/Win Guidelines: Showcasing Conflict Resolution Skills."

9. Say, "Now we're going to act out conflict situations and find solutions even when the other person may not be committed."

a. Distribute copies of the Win/Win Guidelines.

b. Ask the students if anyone has a real conflict which they would like to playact with others in the class. Allow several students to describe their conflicts. Choose one to re-enact.

c. Have the student describe the particular conflict. Do not use the real names of people involved. Children can say, "my friend" or "someone I know."

d. Choose students to play the different parts. Have the student whose conflict it is quietly and briefly go over the "roles" with the players.

e. Ask the players to go to the center of the circle and act out the conflict as it was, including the way in which it was actually concluded.

f. Discuss the feelings of the participants. Discuss why the outcome didn't work. Ask, "Who lost?"

g. Now replay the conflict using the Win/Win Guidelines. Guide the students through each stage. It is the role of the teacher to coach the students each time they role play using the Win/Win Guidelines. You do not have to have your students memorize them. Instead, through repeated playacting, coaching, and reinforcement, they will eventually assimilate the guidelines.

h. Discuss the Win/Win role play. How did the players feel? Ask, "What are the advantages to using Win/Win Guidelines?"

i. Homework: "Tell your family about the Win/Win Guidelines." Say, "Hang them up where everyone in the house can see them. Ask your family if they will try using the guidelines in their next conflict."

THE WIN/WIN GUIDELINES

1. Take time for cooling off if needed. Find alternative ways to express anger.

2. Each person states their feelings and the problem as they see it using "I messages." No blaming, no name-calling, no interrupting.

3. Each person states the problem as the *other person* sees it.

4. Each person says how they themselves are responsible for the problem.

5. Brainstorm solutions together and choose a solution that satisfies both — a Win/Win solution.

6. Affirm your partner.

REFLECTIVE LISTENING

OBJECTIVES

- The children will utilize the technique of reflective listening to solve problems.

- The children will gain a deeper understanding of the importance of listening to others.

    NOTE: This lesson will prepare children to do Step 3 in the Win/Win Guidelines: "Each person states the problem as the other person sees it."

MATERIALS

- Win/Win Guidelines
- Reflective Listening Poster:

REFLECTIVE LISTENING

Reflective listening is listening with complete attention to the person speaking and repeating back in your own words what they just said. When people are listened to in this way they feel affirmed, and they listen better to you when it's your turn to speak.

- Paper, pencils, crayons

PROCEDURE

1. Ask the students to sit in a circle. Say, "In order to get relaxed today, we're going to image pizza. Close your eyes and smell the pizza coming out of the oven. There's steam rising from it. The whole room smells like warm, delicious pizza. Now, pick up a piece. Be careful, it's hot. Take a bite. Picture the cheese stretching out like a long string. Put the long stretch of cheese in your mouth. Now chew. Take another bite. Your mouth feels warm and wonderful. Feel the warm pizza going into your stomach. Now finish that piece and take another. Keep eating the pizza until you're absolutely satisfied. Now have a nice cold drink."

2. Say, "Now open your eyes and keep that warm satisfied feeling inside you. Let that feeling help you to be calm and better able to listen, because today's lesson is about a special way of listening called reflective listening."

3. Say, "Reflective listening is something that we'll be doing when we do the Win/Win Guidelines." Go over the guidelines briefly and then direct the children's attention to Step 3: "Each person states the problem as the other person sees it." Say, "Today's lesson will help

us to do that through a new way of listening."

4. Ask, "How do you feel when someone listens to you?" Discuss.

5. Show the "Reflective Listening" poster. Have a number of students read it aloud to the group.

6. Say, "Now we're going to practice reflective listening."

7. Say, "Each of us is going to have a chance to listen and be listened to. Learning reflective listening is like learning to ride a bike. At first it feels unfamiliar and may be a little hard. The more you do it the more natural it becomes, until it's part of your life." Pick a volunteer to help you model reflective listening.

8. Ask your volunteer to tell you what he/she likes to do best after school. Repeat back in your own words what the student said. Next you tell the student your favorite thing to do after school and have him/her repeat it back. Choose one or two more volunteers and repeat this process before going on to the next one.

9. PROCESS A: "We're going to do two processes using reflective listening. Turn to a

person next to you. One of you will be 'one' and the other 'two.' 'One' will begin by telling 'two' his or her favorite things to do. When I say time, 'two' will repeat it back. Begin." Then switch roles, having "two" tell and "one" repeat back.

10. Ask, "How did it feel to be listened to fully?" Discuss. "Did you prefer listening or being listened to?" Discuss. "How do you think reflective listening can help in working out our conflicts?"

11. PROCESS B: Say, "Now I'm going to ask a question that I want everyone to think about. We're going to go around the circle and everyone will answer the question, but before they do, they must repeat what the person before them said."

> EXAMPLE: Ask the question, "Should kids get homework? Why or why not?" The teacher answers the question first: "Yes, kids should get homework because it helps them learn." Amy is next in the circle. She turns to the teacher, looks directly at the teacher, and says, "You think kids should get homework because it helps them learn." At this point the teacher says, "Yes" because Amy reflected the statement correctly. If Amy had not, the teacher would have said, "No," and Amy would have had to try again. Now, Amy gets to give her answer to the question. She says, "No, kids shouldn't get homework because it's boring." Jason is sitting next to her so he has to reflect back what Amy said before giving his answer. Continue around the circle until each child has had a turn to both reflect what the previous person has said and to give his/her own response.

12. After each child has spoken, discuss the process with the group. Ask, "Was it easy or hard to reflect back what someone else said?"

13. Say, "Knowing reflective listening will help us do the Step 3 of the Win/Win Guidelines, where you state how your partner feels."

14. Follow-up activity: children respond in writing to the following questions: How does it feel when someone really listens to me? Why is it important to listen to others?" Young children can draw a picture which expresses how they feel when they are truly listened to.

> NOTE: Repeat the reflective listening exercise as often as possible, using different questions that children can answer and reflect back to one another.

CREATIVE BRAINSTORMING

OBJECTIVES

- The children will apply the process of brainstorming.

- The children will understand that brainstorming is a creative process that has limitless applications.

- The children will be able to apply this process later, as it applies to the Win/Win Guidelines.

MATERIALS

- A pencil

- Rules for Brainstorming Poster:

> ### RULES FOR BRAINSTORMING
>
> 1. Say anything that comes to mind.
>
> 2. Don't judge your ideas or the ideas of others.
>
> 3. Don't limit your ideas by trying to have them make sense. Invite your mind to be absolutely creative.
>
> 4. Allow your thoughts to come quickly. Let them flow.
>
> 5. Know that people use only a small part of their brains. Brainstorming enables you to unlock the parts you don't ordinarily use. Surprise yourself with new ideas.
>
> 6. See how many creative ideas and solutions you can come up with, and don't restrict your thoughts in any way.
>
> 7. Be outrageous and have fun!

- Chart paper — A large sheet for each group of four or five children

- Markers

  NOTE: Younger children will need the assistance of one aide or helper for each group to record brainstorming ideas.

PROCEDURE

1. State, "We've talked about conflict and conflict resolution. Can you restate what a conflict is?" Discuss. "What does conflict resolution mean?" Discuss. "Is conflict a normal part of human interaction? Do we have a choice in the way we manage our conflicts?" Discuss. "Do you think it's possible to work out differences even if the other person isn't committed to doing so?" Discuss.

2. Say, "Part of working out differences is coming up with ideas for solutions that satisfy all people involved. One way to do this is through the process of brainstorming." Ask if anyone has ever done brainstorming. If so, ask

them to explain the process. If not, tell the class that brainstorming is a creative thought process in which people come up with as many ideas as possible for a topic.

3. Say, "Today we're going to engage in a class brainstorming exercise, and the purpose will be to come up with as many uses as possible for a pencil. The rules for brainstorming are listed on this poster." Hold up the poster and go over the rules carefully.

4. Hold up a pencil, "I want you to think of all the different possible uses for this pencil. Your answers can be silly, outrageous, realistic, unrealistic, common sense, nonsensical, useful, or useless. The whole point is not to limit your thinking. Any thought or idea that comes to you is OK."

5. Say, "We're going to divide into groups of four or five for this process. Choose a group leader [this is where your helper is needed] who will record everybody's responses on chart paper that I will hand out." Pass out paper and markers. "Remember, don't make fun of anyone else's ideas. Everything is acceptable. Also, you're going to have to think fast. I'm going to give you only four minutes. Try to come up with as many ideas as you can. Any questions?"

> NOTE: Younger children can do this as a class activity with the teacher recording brainstorming ideas.

6. Time the activity. Give the class exactly four minutes. At the end, have each group leader read the complete list.

7. Discuss the process. Note if the children's thinking shifted out of the realm of the conventional. Acknowledge them about this, and let them know that brainstorming holds the key to solutions for many different problems and challenges. Say, "There are limitless possibilities that the process of brainstorming unlocks."

8. Ask, "What are some of the different ways we can use brainstorming?" Discuss.

9. Say, "Brainstorming helps us think of solutions to conflicts where we think there are very few, or even none."

10. Say, "How can our world leaders use this process?" Discuss.

BRAINSTORMING SOLUTIONS TO CONFLICTS

OBJECTIVES

The children will "image" various conflict situations and describe them.

- The children will apply the brainstorming technique to generate possible solutions to conflict situations.

- The children will apply the Win/Win Guidelines.

MATERIALS

- Rules for Brainstorming poster (see Lesson 10)

- Chart paper for recording students' brainstorming suggestions

- Chart: Win/Win Guidelines from Lesson 8

PROCEDURE

1. Have the children form a circle. Say, "Today we're going to focus on personal conflicts and we're going to use the process of brainstorming to come up with as many possible solutions as we can."

2. Ask, "Who has had a conflict they would like to discuss with the class? Remember not to use anyone's full name."

3. Select a few children to describe their conflicts.

4. Choose one conflict on which to focus.

5. Ask the children to play act the conflict as it was.

6. Now "re-play" the conflict, using the Win/Win Guidelines. Stop when you get to "brainstorm solutions." Have the role players sit down.

7. Ask the entire class to generate as many solutions as possible. Write them down on chart paper.

8. After you have exhausted every possibility, guide the children to choose several solutions. Circle them on the chart. Encourage the class to be creative with these solutions by either combining them or suggesting their use in different ways.

9. Have the class vote on one solution. Write it on the board.

10. Remind the class that conflict resolution is a creative effort. Say, "Sometimes we don't see the solution to a conflict right away. Problem solving takes time, creativity, and the willingness to come up with ideas we wouldn't ordinarily think of."

NOTE: This process can be repeated in a condensed version several times a week. Take ten minutes at the end of the day, and generate solutions to conflicts within the room. You'll be amazed at how engaged the class becomes in the process. Bring the Win/Win Guidelines and Rules for Brainstorming to a faculty meeting. Offer your colleagues the opportunity to work out their differences, using these techniques. They'll thank you.

TAKING CARE OF OUR EARTH

OBJECTIVES

- Children will actively demonstrate "peace means taking care of our earth," by cleaning up their school yard and planting flower bulbs.

- The children will understand that we are all responsible for taking care of the world around us; each person who takes responsibility makes a big difference even if it's on a small scale.

MATERIALS

- Sign: "Peace Means Taking Care of Ourselves, Each Other, and Our Earth"

- Large poster to be filled in during the lesson entitled "Ways We Can Take Care of Our Earth"

- Trash bags, a flower bulb for each child and old spoons or gardening shovels. If there is no yard around your school, use flower pots or window boxes.

- A picture of the type of flower that will grow from the bulbs (optional)

PROCEDURE

1. Have the children sit in a circle. Say, "Earlier, we learned how to affirm one another by telling each other something special about each other. Today we're going to affirm the earth by taking care of it in a special way." Refer to the sign, "Peace means..."

2. Ask, "What does it mean to take care of our earth?" Discuss.

3. Ask, "How can we take care of our earth? Can you think of some different ways we can do this?" List the children's answers on the chart entitled, "Ways We Can Take Care of Our Earth."

4. Ask the children how they can take care of the area around their school. Discuss.

5. Say, "How would our neighborhood look if everyone took care of it?" Discuss.

6. Say, "How would the world be if everyone all over took care of it? How might it be different?" Discuss.

7. Say, "Today we're going to take care of the area around our school by cleaning it up and planting flower bulbs." Show the bulbs and utensils. Show the picture of the flowers that

will grow from the bulbs. Take the children outside.

8. Pass out the bulbs and trash bags. Have the children work in groups to clean and plant.

9. After you're finished, come back inside and plan your spring planting project. Have the children decide what they're going to plant in the spring (vegetables, flowers, trees).

10. Pick a date on which to do your spring planting and clean-up. Mark it on the calendar.

11. Ask the children how they like taking care of their earth. Ask why it's important to do this. Ask how the children are making a contribution by taking care of the earth. Acknowledge them for doing so.

TAKING CARE OF PEOPLE IN OUR COMMUNITY

NOTE: Prior to this lesson, arrange for a representative from a senior citizen home to speak to the class.

OBJECTIVES

- The children will meet and talk to the representative of a senior citizen's home or center in your community.

- The children will find out ways they can help the senior citizens of your community.

- The children will determine a course of action they can take as a group to work with the senior citizens.

MATERIALS

- Pamphlets or brochures from a local senior citizen's center and pictures of some of the seniors from that center, if possible.

- Chart paper (to be filled in later) entitled, "Our Project for the Senior Citizen's Center" (you can put in the actual name of the center).

PROCEDURE

1. Have the children sit in a circle. Introduce the representative from the senior citizen's center.

2. Have each child introduce him/herself by going around the circle.

3. Ask the representative to tell the children about the center and those who attend or live at the center. Brochures can be passed out at this time.

4. Allow the children to ask questions. They may also want to talk about their own grandparents or other seniors they know.

5. Ask the representative to tell the children about ways they might be helpful to the people in the center. Have the children give their own suggestions.

6. Ask, "How can the senior citizens be helpful to us?" Discuss this and allow the children to come up with suggestions too. Guide the children to see that as people grow older they still have a valuable contribution to make to others, especially by virtue of their knowledge and experience. Let them know that in some cultures, older people are revered.

7. Together, pick a project that the children can do with the senior citizens. The project can be mutually helpful, such as inviting a senior into the class to give extra help to those who need it. At the same time, the children can write letters to "Senior Pen Pals," letting them know about their school, families, and the peacemaking program they are involved in. If your school will allow it, make arrangements every so often for the children to visit the senior citizen's home. They can read to the senior citizens and the seniors can read to them. Or they can bake a treat and bring it in to share. There are many things you can do. Have the children decide, and fill in the chart paper, "Our Project for the Senior Citizen's Center."

8. Write a note home to the children's parents (or have the children do this) and tell them about your project.

9. Ask the children how this project reflects the definition of peace they learned, "Peace means taking care of ourselves, each other, and our earth."

TAKING CARE OF THOSE WHO ARE HUNGRY

NOTE: This lesson should be done before Thanksgiving.

OBJECTIVES

• The children will learn that there are many hungry people in our world, and that they can help.

• The children will understand that having a peaceful world means taking care of one another, not just oneself.

• The children will plan a mini-food drive to collect non-perishables for families who would otherwise not have enough to eat at Thanksgiving.

MATERIALS

• A current events article dealing with the issue of hunger for you to read to the class.

• Poster: "Peace Means Taking Care of Ourselves, Each Other, and Our Earth."

• Notes to parents (see Page 57).

PROCEDURE

1. Have the children form a circle. Say, "Imagine getting up in the morning and not having any food to eat. You get to school and you are hungry but you don't want to tell your teacher about it. You try to do your work but you can't concentrate. You feel tired, and you wish you could put your head down. Lunch time comes, and there's still nothing for you to eat. Your stomach begins to hurt. All you can think about is food but there isn't any."

2. Give the children about three minutes of silence to imagine this. Ask them to open their eyes and say, "How did you feel during the imagery process?" Discuss. Be especially sensitive to those children in your class who may have experienced or are experiencing feelings similar to those described in the imagery process.

3. Tell the children that there are many hungry people in the world and the majority of them are children.

> NOTE: The Hunger Project has an excellent school in-service program. If you would like an in-depth presentation on

ending hunger for your class, you can arrange for a presentation by writing the following address: The Hunger Project, 2015 Steiner Street, San Francisco, Calif. 94115

4. Tell the children that hunger does not have to exist, and that they can begin to alleviate it right in their own communities.

5. Ask the children what they would like to do to help end hunger in their community. Discuss.

6. Read the current events article on hunger. Discuss it.

7. Ask the class to begin collecting canned and dry goods to be given to hungry people at Thanksgiving. You can arrange for the food to be distributed (and possibly even picked up) through one of your local churches or civic organizations.

8. Refer to the poster, "Peace Means Taking Care of Ourselves, Each Other and Our Earth." Ask the children how their involvement in ending hunger relates to the words on the poster. Discuss.

9. Distribute the letters to parents. Go over them with the class.

10. See if your students or parents would like to expand the project. Perhaps a parent would like to organize the planning of a Thanksgiving dinner to be delivered to a needy family. What other ideas does the class have? Perhaps you'd like to involve another class, perhaps the entire school: The sky's the limit on contribution.

LETTER TO PARENTS

Lesson 14
Taking Care of Those Who Are Hungry

Dear Parents,

As Thanksgiving draws near we are reminded of those people who may not be well provided for this year. Our class is collecting canned and dried goods to be given to those in need this Thanksgiving. Could you send in an unopened can or box of non-perishable food for this purpose? Your help will be appreciated by many people.

Do you have any other ideas? If you would like to help us expand our project, please let us know. Thanks for being there.

Much love,

Student's Name

THE BASIC NEEDS OF PEOPLE

OBJECTIVES

- The children will discover that all people have the same basic needs, and that we are all the same inside.

- The children will understand the basic needs we all share are: food, clothing, shelter, and love.

- The children will understand that regardless of how people look, act, and live, their basic needs are the same.

MATERIALS

- Chart with the words "Basic Needs of People" hand-lettered on top

- Markers

- National Geographic magazines or other magazines and posters with pictures of people from different cultures

- A globe

- Chart paper with the words: "Ways in Which All People Are Alike" hand-lettered on top

PROCEDURE

1. Have the children sit in a circle. Affirm them by reminding them that they are each special and unique. Tell them that everyone on earth has something special about them. Tell them also that we share something with all the people on earth — our basic needs. Have a chart paper hanging in front of the room with the title: "Basic Needs of People." Ask the children to look at the chart.

2. Ask, "What are things or conditions that you need for survival?" (Define survival.) Determine through discussion the differences between needs and wants. Stress that needs are things or conditions we must have in order to live. Wants are optional and do not determine our survival.

3. Have your students state "needs" as you list them on the chart. The basic needs are: food, clothing, shelter and love. Things connected to these four basics such as medicine, money, etc. can also be included. However, a clear distinction must be made between what people need and want.

4. Show pictures of people from other cultures. Ask, "Do you suppose these people have the same needs as we do?" Discuss. Guide your students to the conclusion that regardless of how differently people look, live, act or speak —

they all have the same basic needs. Children can locate countries on the globe where people in the pictures come from.

5. Focus on the pictures again. Ask, "How are these people different from you? How are they like you?" Ask, "When people look different does that mean their basic needs are different from yours?" Discuss.

6. Focus on pictures of different environmental settings including people in native dress, their homes, families, and foods. Ask, "What basic needs are being met in these pictures?"

7. Say, "Even though people of other cultures may look different from us, in what specific ways are they like us?" List similarities on chart entitled: Ways in Which All People Are Alike.

8. Ask, "If someone does look different, does that mean they are different inside?" Discuss.

9. Tell the children that conflicts are often based on perceived differences (racial, gender, cultural, religious, handicaps). Discuss.

10. Say, "Sometimes differences are perceived as threatening." Explain that sometimes we don't trust people who look and act differently from us. Say, "Sometimes wars have been fought over differences. The important thing to remember is that the basic needs of people are

the same no matter how different they appear to be. We are all interconnected." Define the word interconnected. Say, "We are the 'human family.' It's important to care about other people not just about those who are like us. We live on this earth together (indicate wholeness of globe). We will always be connected as inhabitants of the same planet. Having a peaceful world means accepting each other and knowing we're the same inside, and that we all need the same things. It's also important to remember that all people are special."

11. Ask, "Do you ever find it hard to accept people who seem too different from you?" Discuss.

12. Ask, "Have you ever not been accepted by someone else because they thought you were different?" Discuss.

13. Ask, "If peace starts with you, how do you need to treat others, especially those people who appear to be different?" Discuss. Conclude the lesson with an affirmation of the children. Let them know that they are capable of accepting differences even though it might feel hard to do this at times.

WE ARE ALL INTERCONNECTED

OBJECTIVES

- The children will demonstrate the understanding that all people have the same basic needs (food, clothing, shelter, love).

- The children will understand that when people are committed to solving conflicts, they can find ways to resolve them.

- The children will understand that they can change the way they perceive differences by remembering that people all over the world are the same inside and are interconnected (mutually joined or related).

MATERIALS

- Large globe

- A copy of National Geographic or other magazine depicting a lifestyle different from our own (e.g., Africa, India, China)

- Piece of clay, string, or yarn

- Yardsticks or long piece of string to use as a "boundary"

- Any photograph depicting war or physical conflict

PROCEDURE

1. Have the children sit in a circle on the floor. Place the globe in the center of the circle.

2. Review the concept that people all over the world need food, clothing, shelter, and love. Show a picture to the children depicting people in a country where the lifestyle is visibly different from their own.

3. Ask the students to look carefully at the picture and to describe how the people are different in the way they live, dress, or look. When appropriate, read descriptive excerpts from the magazine you have chosen. Encourage full participation. Your students may conclude that the houses shown are different because of the climate and the terrain, and that social activities may be different because of the different available facilities. Phrase your questions so the children can begin to hypothesize, draw conclusions, and use creative and critical thinking. Try to get them to draw on their own experience and on facts they may have learned before this lesson, as well as from this new material.

4. Guide your students to consider the similarities between the people in the pictures and people in the United States. Focus on basic human needs as one commonality we all share, regardless of differences.

5. Guide the children to reiterate that all people have the basic needs of food, clothing, shelter — and love.

6. Using the globe, place a small clay ball as a marker on the country depicted in the picture. Place another on the United States. Connect the two with a small piece of string or yarn. Stress the concept that all people are "interconnected." Define. Ask the children what "interconnected" means to them.

7. Have your students look at the globe. Say, "Astronauts in outer space see the earth as one unit. They also see the earth with no boundaries between nations. In seeing the earth this way, people are reminded that we share one earth; we are all interconnected. Different people in different nations are part of one human family." Explain the meaning of the word boundaries.

8. Using pictures of battle scenes, discuss how people in different lands have fought over boundaries. Ask the children what sometimes happens when people of one country cross over the boundaries of an enemy country. Discuss.

9. Have your students playact such a situation. Separate one part of the room from the other with yardsticks or string. Choose children to play the parts of leaders of different countries over which there is a "border" dispute. Ask the class to think of ways the dispute can be settled. Discuss. Repeat the role play using the Win/Win Guidelines.

Stress the fact that sometimes people forget that they're all the same inside, especially during times of disagreement. But the fact remains, people are all the same inside, and that we do have the ability to work out our differences. Say, "Sometimes this seems impossible to us. We get discouraged and feel that we can't settle things peacefully. Sometimes we don't want to settle things peacefully, especially when we're angry. It's the same for our governments. All those feelings are natural. Just remember, we always have a choice in the way we work out our problems."

10. Ask, "What generally happens when you hit someone?" The children will probably respond by saying, "They hit me back." Ask, "Then what do you do?" Guide the children to see that one person hitting another usually escalates into a fight. Define the word escalate. Let the children know that the same thing happens with nations. Say, "When one nation 'hurts' another, and the other nation 'hurts' them back, what can this develop into?" Ask, "How can we prevent this from happening?" Be sure to draw the relationship between individual and global acts. Continue to stress the idea that we always have a choice in the way we act, and choosing hurtful actions usually causes more of the same.

WHAT IS A PEACEMAKER

OBJECTIVES

- The children will understand the qualities of a peacemaker.

- The children will identify times they have been peacemakers.

- The children will understand that peacemaking is not always easy, and that it's important not to give up when we get discouraged.

MATERIALS

- Large chart with the following information:

> A PEACEMAKER IS SOMEONE WHO:
>
> - cares about and accepts others
> - cares about and accepts him/herself
> - is patient
> - helps and affirms others
> - is creative and tries to come up with solutions even when there don't seem to be any
> - can change his/her mind (is flexible)
> - has a vision
> - has many different feelings including anger, but tries his or her best to work out conflicts peacefully
> - is committed enough to try to work things out even when discouraged
> - is forgiving

- A small teacher- or child-made picture of the planet earth

PROCEDURE

1. Ask the children to form a circle. Show the chart "A Peacemaker Is Someone Who." Have the students read the qualities.

2. Ask, "When have you exhibited any of these qualities?" Lead the discussion with your own personal anecdote.

3. Have the children think of a time when they exhibited any of the qualities on the chart. Discuss.

4. Say, "Close your eyes and picture yourself at a time when you exhibited one or more of the qualities of a peacemaker." Reread the chart. Say, "Picture yourself as a peacemaker. Who are you with? What are you doing? What are you

saying? How do you feel? Try to recreate that feeling now." Give students about two to three minutes to do this.

5. Say, "We're going to pass the picture of the planet earth around the circle. When you hold it I'd like you to share your experience of being a peacemaker. The picture of the earth reminds us that we are all part of one planet, and that each individual is important."

6. Pass around the picture of the earth. Encourage each child to share a time in which he or she exhibited at least one quality of a peacemaker. Acknowledge each child warmly, thanking each for participating.

7. Ask, "Is it sometimes hard to be a peace-maker?" Discuss.

8. Share a time when it was hard for you to be a peacemaker.

9. Ask, "Are there times you don't want to be a peacemaker?" Discuss and share a time when you haven't wanted to be a peacemaker yourself.

10. Tell the children that it's human nature to not get along all the time — to be so angry at times that we don't want to make up. State, "The thing to remember is that we always have a choice, and things usually work out better when we choose to be peaceful. That doesn't mean that we have to allow others to be mean or hurtful toward us. What it means is that we try to understand why the other person is acting that way; we try to ask ourselves what else we can do besides being hurtful too."

11. Affirm the children by thanking them for their honesty and willingness to think about these questions.

THINGS I'M GOOD AT

OBJECTIVES

- The children will learn to create a peaceful feeling within.
- The children will identify several different things they are good at.
- The children will draw or write and discuss things they are good at, reinforcing positive self-esteem.

MATERIALS

- Puppet or "I'm Good At" sign (optional)
- Tape recorder and blank tape
- Drawing paper and lined writing paper, crayons

    NOTE: This lesson correlates with Bulletin Board 2 entitled "Things I'm Good At."

PROCEDURE

1. Have the students sit in a circle with legs crossed.

2. Say, "We're going to get very relaxed today before beginning our lesson. We're going to create a peaceful, quiet feeling in our classroom and within ourselves."

3. Say, "Close your eyes, and let your feet feel perfectly relaxed and tingly. Now let the tingly, relaxed feeling go into your legs, body, arms, hands, neck, face, and head. Breathe slowly and feel the quiet in your bodies." Give the children a moment or two of complete silence. When this is complete, tell the children that, whenever they need to, they can bring back that relaxed feeling by themselves, simply by recreating the "tingly feeling" from their toes to their heads.

4. Now, ask them to picture their mind as a blank movie screen as they did in Lesson 2. Have them picture themselves on the screen doing something they're good at. Suggest different things they like: sports activities; dance; singing; art; cooking; reading; helping people; figuring out solutions. Younger children can be encouraged to think also about dressing themselves, making their bed, tying their shoelaces, etc.

5. Say, "Now watch yourself doing something you're good at. Most of us are good at many different things, so choose only one for now. How do you look doing the thing you're good at? How do you feel? How do other people feel

about you when you're doing this?" Give the children time to think and envision themselves quietly.

6. After a few moments, ask the children to open their eyes and share. Briefly reiterate the Guidelines for Sharing from Lesson 2, no put-downs, etc. Begin the sharing time with your own vision.

7. It's fun to use a puppet with younger children during this lesson; e.g., "Big Bird" might say, "I'm good at helping my friend tie his shoelaces." Pass the puppet around the circle, allowing each child that can use it to say "I'm good at...." With older children, use an "I'm Good At" sign which each child can hold on his or her turn. Tape record the children speaking.

8. After each child has had a turn, have the class return to their seats and draw and/or write about themselves doing the thing they're good at. For young children, the teacher can write: "[name] is good at [activity]" on top of each child's paper. Older children can do this independently. Play back the tape while the children draw and write.

9. To conclude the lesson, have the children share their pictures and/or stories with one another in small groups and discuss.

Bulletin Board 2
Learning the Skills of Peacemaking

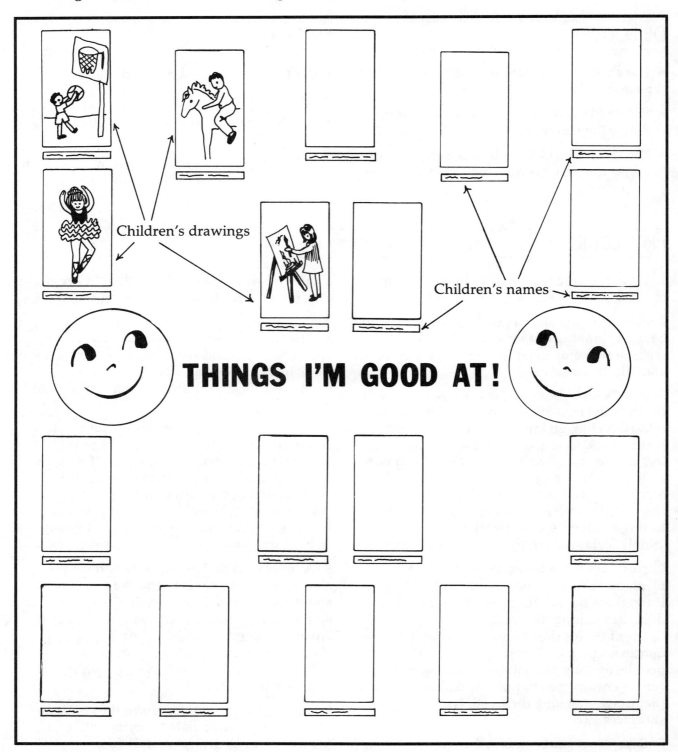

Children's drawings

Children's names

THINGS I'M GOOD AT!

INTRODUCING PEACEMAKING JOURNALS

OBJECTIVES

- The children will learn the process of journaling.

- The children will understand the purpose of their peacemaking journal.

- The children will draw and write their vision of a peaceful classroom.

MATERIALS

- Children's Journals — black and white composition notebooks for older children. Notebooks with blank paper for younger children

- Teacher's Journal (keeping your own Peacemaking Journal is an essential part of the process)

- Peacemaking Journal Box — a large cardboard box, covered to your taste and labeled

PROCEDURE

1. Prior to this lesson, have each child bring in the notebook which will serve as his/her Peacemaking Journal throughout the year. Tell the class that you will be discussing many new ideas this year, and that the journal will serve three purposes:

- It will be a place where each child can express his/her thoughts and feelings on specific topics

- It will be a place where each child can express thoughts whenever they come up in all areas of peacemaking

- It will be a place in which to discover solutions to problems through writing or drawing

2. Show your journal to the class. Explain that you will be journaling along with them, and from time to time you will read your journal entries to the class. Explain that the process of peacemaking is something new and that you will all be learning about it together. Say, "You will also learn about yourselves through the process of journaling."

3. Ask the children if any of them ever has kept any kind of journal before. Ask if they know the purpose of journal-keeping (self-knowledge). Discuss. Tell your class that the more people learn about themselves, the better they relate to

the people around them. State: "Having a world at peace means relating well to ourselves and others. The journal process helps this happen."

4. Tell your class, "The most important thing in journal writing is to freely express your ideas without judging them. Whatever you write will be fine. Spelling, neatness, and grammar don't count. The only thing that matters is letting your ideas flow." Discuss. Some children may be concerned that they won't have any ideas, or that their ideas won't be good enough. Allow them to express their concerns, and assure them that there is no right or wrong way to express oneself in journaling. Say, "Our minds are filled with thoughts, ideas, and feelings. The journal is the place where we can bring all of this out of our minds and onto paper."

5. Show your class the Peacemaking Journal Box. Tell them that they will put their journals in this box after each entry, and then the journals will be returned to them. Say, "If you want to express ideas, thoughts, or feelings at any time, you can write in your journal and place it in the box for me to read."

6. State, "Now we're going to do our first journal entry. The topic is 'My Vision of a Peaceful Classroom.' We're going to do an imagery process which will unblock your thoughts and help bring out ideas to put into

your journal."

7. State, "Close your eyes and picture our classroom being empty. This is the beginning of a new day. It's bright and sunny, and you feel wonderful. Now fill the room with children, and have them treating each other in a way that makes everyone feel accepted and at home. Picture all the children being together in this way. What does it feel like? How do you feel? What are you learning about in this classroom? What do you most want to learn about? Change the bulletin boards and room decorations if you like. What does it look like? How do you feel coming to school in this kind of classroom?" Have the children picture their images in silence for a few moments.

8. State, "Open your eyes and write down what you just pictured." Drawing is appropriate for young children. "Describe what you saw, how you felt, what the other people were doing. Anything you write is fine."

9. Give the class five to ten minutes to work. Older children can draw in their journals, also. Say, "If you have a picture in your mind to go along with what you are writing, draw it on the opposite page."

10. Ask the class if anyone would like to share their journal entries with the class. Let them know that they don't ever have to share their journal entries. Remind your students that there are no put-downs or negative comments of any kind about other people's journal entries. Say, "Peace begins within each of us. Accepting others and what others have to say is a big part of this."

11. Discuss the journal entries together. Have the children place their journals in the box each time they have made an entry. Return them with your responses when appropriate.

JOURNAL LESSON: FEELING SPECIAL

OBJECTIVES

- The children will apply techniques of journaling.
- The children will use the process of imagery in the journal process.
- The children will recall a time they felt special, thereby building self-esteem.

MATERIALS

- Teacher's journal
- Journals, pencils, pens, crayons
- Peacemaking Journal Box

PROCEDURE

1. Have the children sit in a circle. Say, "You had your first experience in journal writing during our last lesson. Is there anyone who didn't read his or her last journal entry aloud last time who would like to do so now? This is entirely optional." Young children can describe their drawings.

2. Tell the children that no judgements or criticisms are to be made on anyone's entries. Allow time for brief discussion.

3. Say, "Today we're going to focus on something new in our journals."

4. Say, "Remember, a journal usually describes someone's feelings, thoughts, or responses. The best journals are those in which the writer expresses his/her feelings freely. When you journal, allow your feelings to flow out of you, and write them down exactly the way they are. Also remember spelling, grammar, and neatness are not important in journaling. The most important thing is that you express your thoughts and feelings."

5. State, "Each of you is a special and unique individual. You are an important part of the world in which we live. Each of you has the ability to make a huge difference in the world, and your thoughts are very important. Respect your own thoughts. They are a special part of you."

6. Say, "Now we're going to do a journal exercise in which we will use our imaginations to recall a time we felt special or important."

7. Say, "Let's get relaxed. Let your body become very still and quiet. Close your eyes and listen to the calmness in the room. Take a deep breath in through your nose and out through your mouth. Now recall the smell of a flower. Breathe in deeply and smell the fragrance. Let the fragrance go deep inside of you. Breathe in again and allow the beautiful fragrance of the flower to move throughout your entire body. Now just let your body relax and imagine that the whole room is filled with the fragrance of your flower."

8. State, "Keep your eyes closed. I'm going to ask you to recall a time when you felt special or important. It can be a time when you may have helped another person, or a time when you were given a new responsibility, a time when you learned to do something new, or any other time when you felt special. Keep your eyes closed and picture yourself doing whatever you were doing at the time. How did you feel? How did you look? Picture the expression on your face, the position of your body. Recall the thoughts you had about yourself when you were feeling so special. Recapture that feeling again now." Give the children one to two minutes of silence.

9. State, "Open your eyes. How do you feel?" Allow children to share.

10. Ask, "Who would like to share about the time you just recalled, a time of feeling special and important?" Allow the children time to share. You can share first.

11. Ask, "Is there anyone who had difficulty recalling a time of feeling special or important?" If anyone says yes, offer to speak to that child privately at a later time if he/she wishes. Do a little "coaching," and see if you can help to bring about some positive recollection.

12. State, "Now we're going to write in our journals what we just recalled in our imaginations. (Younger children will draw.) Be descriptive. Write (draw) about your feelings, the situation, how you reacted and what it was like. Allow the feelings to guide your pen (crayon). Don't be afraid of making mistakes. There are no mistakes in journaling." If there are one or two who couldn't recall a time of feeling special or important, now is the time to speak with them privately.

13. Allow students about ten minutes of silence in which to write or draw. Children who write and finish early can draw a picture to go along with their entry, start a new entry on a topic they choose, or read a book.

14. Ask the children to place their journals in the box at the end of the lesson.

15. Journal entries can be discussed the following day.

PEACEMAKER OF THE WEEK

OBJECTIVES

- The students who have applied the Win/Win Guidelines and who have exhibited the qualities of a peacemaker will receive recognition for their efforts and actions.

- The students will evaluate their own and each others' actions according to how well they exemplify peacemaking behavior.

MATERIALS

- Peacemaker of the Week Award Certificate (devise your own format using this suggested wording:

  "[Name] has been named Peacemaker of the Week for [Deed].

  Each person can make a difference in the world.

  We honor [Name] for taking the responsibility to affect others in a positive way."

- Win/Win Guidelines poster from Lesson 8 for review

- "A Peacemaker Is Someone Who" chart from Lesson 17 for review

- 5" X 8" file box or any similar box for peacemaker nominations, labeled, "Peacemaker of the Week."

- Notecards

  NOTE: This lesson corresponds with the "Peacemakers of the Week" bulletin board at the end of this lesson.

PROCEDURE

1. Have the class sit in a circle on the floor.

2. Say, "I'd like you to close your eyes and find a peaceful place inside. In that place, think about the way you treated people this week. Think about your friends in school, your family, people on your block, or people you don't know that well. Think about a time this week when you acted like a peacemaker. You may have used the Win/Win Guidelines to work out a problem, you may have affirmed someone, or you may have helped another person. In your imagination, look at the other person's face and see how he/she feels. Now feel your own feelings. Think about this, and in a moment I'm going to ask you to share your experiences."

3. Have the children open their eyes. Go around the circle giving each child a chance to respond to the statement, "I was a peacemaker when . . ."

4. After sharing, affirm the class. Example: "I want to acknowledge you all for living the words 'Peace begins with me.' Being a peacemaker takes effort and concern. I know you will each make a difference in the world as the result of your efforts."

5. Say, "To recognize how important your efforts as peacemakers are, we are going to start a special program called, 'Peacemakers of the Week.' Each week we will pick two students as the Peacemakers of the Week. One will be

nominated by the students and one will be selected by the teacher. Each will receive this award certificate." (Show sample certificate.) This also can be done with only one student each week.

6. Have a class discussion to devise guidelines for selecting a person for the Peacemaker of the Week Award. Brainstorm as a group the ways a person should act to be selected. Refer to the poster for Win/Win Guidelines and "A Peacemaker Is Someone Who ...."

7. Say, "On a note card, write your name, the date, and the name of someone you feel is a peacemaker in our class. Describe specifically how that person acted as a peacemaker." Do a sample one on the board. Example: "Tommy was a peacemaker when he helped me with my math." Say, "Put the nomination notecard in the Peacemaker of the Week Box. We will use the nominations to select our Peacemakers of the Week."

8. The process you may want to use for student selection is to list on the board the nominations in the box, then have others speak on behalf of the nominations. The selection could then be by private ballot.

9. The teacher can select the second Peacemaker of the Week based on observations of the children throughout the week.

10. End the lesson by selecting two Peacemakers of the Week and awarding them each a certificate.

11. Follow up: Ask students each day if they are thinking of how they and others are acting as peacemakers and whom they will nominate. Do the awarding the same day each week so students can look forward to it. You can provide extra recognition for recipients by asking them to bring a photo of themselves to school to be placed on a "Peacemakers of the Week" bulletin board. You can also keep a "Peacemaker Honor Roll," a permanent list to be hung on this bulletin board, on which each "Peacemaker of the Week" appears.

Bulletin Board 3
Learning the Skills of Peacemaking

PEACEMAKERS OF THE WEEK

PEACEMAKER
HONOR ROLL

A PEACEMAKER
IS SOMEONE WHO . . . .

— CARES ABOUT OTHERS,
ETC.

Construction paper sunshine

Paper border

Photo
(Name)

Photo
(Name)

PEACEMAKERS IN MY LIFE

OBJECTIVES

- The children will review the qualities of a peacemaker.

- The children will identify and describe people they know who exhibit these qualities.

- The children will identify people they've heard about who are peacemakers.

MATERIALS

- A selected story or article about a peacemaker (Martin Luther King, Ghandhi, Rosa Parks, etc.). See resource section for suggested books

- "A Peacemaker Is Someone Who . . ." chart from Lesson 17

- Journals, pencils, crayons

PROCEDURE

1. Have children sit in a circle. Read the story or article describing the peacemaker you have chosen.

2. Refer to the "A Peacemaker Is Someone Who . . ." chart. Ask, "What qualities did this person exhibit?" Discuss.

3. Ask, "What do you admire most about this person?" Discuss.

4. Ask, "How would our world be different if there were more people like _____ ?" Discuss.

5. Say, "Now I'd like you to take a few moments and think about people in your life who are peacemakers. They should be ordinary people — not famous people in the news. Remember, all people who ended up becoming famous peacemakers started off as ordinary people, just like us."

6. Have each child turn to the person he/she is sitting next to. Ask each child to share with his/her partner about the peacemaker they are thinking of.

7. After about four minutes, have the children face forward in the circle. Ask them to describe the peacemaker in their lives, and to tell what qualities they exhibit which make them peacemakers.

8. Say, "Do you think it's ever hard for these people to be peacemakers?" Discuss. Ask, "Do you think they ever get angry and act in ways that aren't peaceful?" Discuss. Ask, "Do you think it's possible to be a peacemaker even if there are times you are not peaceful?" Discuss. Say, "One quality that helps people to be peacemakers is commitment. When you are committed to something, that doesn't mean you never make mistakes. It means you keep trying even after you have made a mistake." Give a personal example.

9. Using the journals, ask the children to draw and/or write a picture and/or story about an ordinary person in their lives whom they think is a peacemaker.

10. Have the children share their stories and pictures and discuss them.

MEASURING THE UNDERSTANDINGS LEARNED IN THIS GUIDE

STAGE I: Peace Begins With Me

NOTE: This page can be used in two different ways. For younger children you can ask the questions aloud as a means of review. This will enable you to find out how much of the content they are absorbing. For older children you can use this page as an informal test to measure the depth of understanding of concepts.

1. What does peace mean to you?

2. What are the qualities of a peacemaker?

3. Which of these qualities have you shown in your own life?

4. What are the Win/Win Guidelines used for?

5. List the Win/Win Guidelines in your own words.

6. How have you applied the Win/Win Guidelines in your life?

7. What is an "I Message"? Give two examples.

8. What does it mean to affirm someone? Give an example.

9. What are the basic needs of people?

10. How can the world be a better place through the use of peacemaking skills?

STAGE II: INTEGRATING PEACEMAKING INTO OUR LIVES

LAO TZU

If there is right in the soul,
There will be beauty in the person;

If there is beauty in the person,
There will be harmony in the home;

If there is harmony in the home,
There will be order in the nation;
If there is order in the nation,
There will be peace in the world.

PEACE STARTS WITH ME

OBJECTIVES

- The children will develop another dimension of understanding how peace starts with the individual.
- The children will develop an understanding that there are different ways people experience peace as individuals.
- The children will develop an understanding that if people want a peaceful home, school, community, world, then it is up to each individual to take responsibility for his/her own interactions.

MATERIALS

- Poster:

WE TAKE CARE OF OUR BODIES BY:
Observing safety rules
Getting proper rest and sleep
Eating healthy foods
Getting proper dental care
Having regular check-ups at the doctor

- Poster:

WE KEEP OUR MINDS HEALTHY BY:
Learning and going to school
Giving ourselves time to rest and relax
Having someone to talk to when we have a problem (mom, dad, friends)
Knowing how to relax when we are under stress
(Describe stress as the nervous, unsettled feeling we get when we're afraid or pressured)

- Drawing paper (for "When I Feel Peaceful, I Look Like This")
- Crayons or markers
- Journals

PROCEDURE

1. Say, "Let's form our circle. We're going to start off with an exercise which will help us to feel calm and peaceful inside. Close your eyes."

2. Say, "Imagine you've just had a cup of hot chocolate with whipped cream on top. Feel yourself drinking it. Feel the warmth going down through your chest, into your stomach. It feels good. As you drink your hot chocolate, feel the warmth spread through your body, making you feel cozy and relaxed. Taste the sweetness in your mouth. Let the warmth spread from your chest and stomach to the rest of your body, your arms, legs, and head. You feel safe

and calm and peaceful. Let the feeling fill your whole body. It's a feeling you can take everywhere you go."

3. State, "Open your eyes now. How do you feel?" Children share. Focus on the quiet, relaxed feelings that the children describe. Discuss these feelings. Have the children give specific descriptions of their calm, peaceful feelings (For example: "My body feels warm and tingly," or "I feel happy inside.")

4. State, "Think of other times you have felt this way. Can you describe them?" Children share their recollections.

5. State, "There are different ways we can feel peaceful inside. As you've described, sometimes pleasant circumstances and events can bring forth that feeling within us. Sometimes we feel that way when we're with special people. In all cases, where do peaceful feelings start?" Guide children to the understanding that peacefulness begins within each individual.

6. Say, "People also tend to feel peaceful when they take care of their well-being." Remind the class that well-being is the state you're in when your mind and body feel healthy and taken care of. Ask, "What are some ways we take care of our bodies?" Refer to the "We Take Care of Our Bodies" poster. Other examples can be added from the children's experiences.

7. Ask, "When our minds are strong and healthy, we have good mental health. How do we take care of our minds?" Responses can be listed on the "We Keep Our Minds Healthy" poster. Ask, "What do you do to relax?" Have the children add to the list.

8. Ask, "When you feel peaceful inside, how do you usually act with others?" Discuss. "When you feel stressful, tense, or frightened, how do you act with others?" Discuss. "Think of a time when your body wasn't at peace, like when you were hurt, or very hungry, or very tired. Did you act any differently with the people around you?"

9. State, "There are three main things to remember about being peaceful inside: (1) We are all responsible for our well-being. We must take proper care of our minds and bodies. (2) When we don't take care of ourselves — for example, if we stay up too late or don't eat properly — we tend not to feel and act peacefully. (3) We always have a choice in the way we act. Even when we don't feel peaceful, a peaceful place still lives inside us. We can choose to act from that place, and to do the things necessary for our health and well-being."

10. State, "Close your eyes again for a moment. Remember the imaging process we did at the beginning of this lesson. Remember how warm and peaceful you felt. Remember other times you felt that way inside. Try to bring that feeling back again. Find the place inside you where that feeling lives. Recreate the peaceful feeling." Children do this for one to two minutes.

11. Ask, "Were you able to bring the feeling back?" Discuss briefly. Stress the fact that all people have the ability to find the peaceful place within. If you practice doing this every day, it will become easier. This exercise can help anyone in the class whenever you feel upset, nervous, or frightened."

12. Ask, "If we want a peaceful home, school community, world, with whom does it begin?" State, "Remember, taking care of ourselves helps us be peaceful. Also, we always have a choice in the way we act with others. As human beings we have the ability to choose peaceful actions, and if we make a mistake, there's always next time. We all make mistakes, and sometimes we disappoint ourselves and others. That doesn't mean there's anything wrong with us. You're still a special person, you've just made a mistake, that's all."

13. Pass out drawing paper. Have children draw pictures and title them, "When I Feel Peaceful I Look Like This." Pictures should also include the people and activities related to the feeling of peacefulness.

14. Allow the children to share and discuss their pictures.

15. Older children can do a related written journal entry. Younger children can continue in their journals by drawing another peaceful situation.

CONNECTING TO THE WORLD AROUND US

NOTE: The Current Events Letter to Parents (Page 88) should be discussed in class and sent home prior to this lesson.

OBJECTIVES

- The children will evaluate a current events article dealing with either peace or the environment.

- The children will draw their own conclusions based on information in the article.

- The children will brainstorm solutions to problems in the article.

- The children will work collaboratively to attempt to reach an agreement.

    NOTE: Younger children will need one aide or helper per brainstorming group.

MATERIALS

- Large poster entitled: "Ways We Become Well-Informed"

- A selected current events article (for the teacher)

- Children's articles

- One large chart-size paper per group of five children

- One magic marker per group

PROCEDURE

1. Have the students form a circle and bring their articles. Say, "Remember the word 'contribution'? What does that mean?" Focus on the meaning of contribution as a way people can give of themselves to those around them, or to society in general.

2. Say, "Can you think of anyone who makes a contribution to the world around us?" Briefly discuss.

3. Say, "One of the ways we can all make a contribution is by being well-informed." Explain the meaning of the word well-informed. Say, "As citizens of our country and of the world, we can stay informed in many different ways. What are some of the ways we stay informed?" List the students' ideas on the "Ways We Become Well-Informed" chart. Examples can be: read the newspapers, listen to the radio, watch the news, have class and family discussions, go places.

4. Say, "You have all become better informed by learning about the news in your articles." Have each student briefly tell the person he or she is sitting next to about his/her article.

5. Say, "Today we're going to inform ourselves about..." [main idea of article you have chosen]. "I am going to read you an article I brought in that we will discuss together. Through group discussion we are going to come up with solutions to the problem addressed in this article."

6. Read the article to the class.

7. Define terms used in the article. It is best to give some background before doing this. Also, articles with pictures engage the children more. With younger children you might have to paraphrase the entire article.

8. Discuss the article.

9. Ask, "What problem is focused on?"

10. Divide the children into "problem-solving groups" of four or five. Tell the students that they will discuss solutions in their groups.

11. Ask the students in each group to choose a leader. Tell the students they must decide on their leader quietly, calmly, peacefully, and quickly. Let them decide how to choose. For young children, the aide or helper will assist at this point.

12. Then ask the students to come up with solutions. Ask "How can we deal with this problem in a way that satisfies the needs of all involved?"

13. Give the students seven to ten minutes to brainstorm ideas, record, and discuss. Circulate and coach.

14. After the allotted time, ask each group to choose one solution to the problem.

15. Give a few more minutes. Tell the students that the agreement must be reached calmly and fairly, so no one loses. Remind them of the Win/Win Guidelines if conflicts arise.

16. After five minutes, see how many groups actually came to an agreement. Ask the group leaders to report on how the agreement was reached, or what caused any lack of agreement.

17. Discuss the dynamics of group interaction and the feelings of the participants.

18. Guide the students to the understanding that agreements in groups are not always easy to reach especially with critical issues. Stress that being a good citizen of the world means working hard and creating solutions even in the face of difficulties. Also stress that there are no easy answers to war and pollution. It is up to all of us to create the solutions.

> NOTE: Some students may become very engaged in the problems focused on in the article. Encourage them to write "Letters to the Editor," or to other people related to the issue, expressing their views. Mail all letters. The following is an example of a letter from a group of first graders.

SAMPLE LETTER
Learning the Skills of Peacemaking
Lesson 24

Dear Friends,

   Let's all try to make peace in the world. Let's try not to fight. We need peace in the world to live. We do not like wars. Wars make lots of people die. We don't want you to die either. We should make friends with each other. We should be nice to all other people. We should love each other. When you fight with your brother and sister, please make friends.
   Please do not fight to live — make peace. We hope we can all be friends. People are nice everywhere!

Love,

The Boys & Girls of Mrs. Drew's Class

   This letter was subsequently sent to a teacher in the USSR. The children also expressed their concerns in letters to the local newspapers. The exercise was a powerful example of the fact that we can all make a difference regardless of our ages.

   NOTE: This lesson can be done repeatedly throughout the year, focusing on different issues.

CURRENT EVENTS LETTER TO PARENTS
Learning the Skills of Peacemaking
Lesson 24

Dear Parents,

Throughout the year our class will be doing current events lessons based on things the children are learning in Learning the Skills of Peacemaking. You can help enormously by doing the following:

a. Provide your child with a newspaper or magazine to look through.
b. Ask your child what kind of article is needed.
c. Assist your child in locating the particular article, if necessary.
d. Make certain the article is appropriate for your child, not frightening or too complex.
e. Read the article with your child and help him or her summarize it orally.
f. Explain unfamiliar terms or ideas.

Today, your child needs a current events article on _____ .
Thanks so much for your help.

Sincerely,

_____
(Teacher's name)

OUR VISIONS ARE SPECIAL

OBJECTIVES

- The children will identify their personal dreams or visions in life.

- The children will "image" and then draw or write their visions.

    NOTE: This lesson correlates with Bulletin Board 4 entitled "Our Visions are Special."

MATERIALS

- Poster:

    > "The first thing about winning is to believe you can do it; after that it takes hard work, determination, and support of others."
    >
    > Wilma Rudolph

- "The Dream of Winning — Wilma Rudolph" (see Page 90)

- Cloud patterns, cotton, paste, 9 X 12 white paper, and crayons or large white paper for freehand drawings

- Tape recorder and blank tape

- Books from the library on Wilma Rudolph (optional)

- Journals, pencils, crayons

PROCEDURE

1. Have the children sit in a circle. Say, "Close your eyes and picture yourself floating on a fluffy white cloud. It feels like cotton yet it's strong enough to hold you. You feel safe and free and happy. This is your cloud. Make it any shape or size you want it to be. Just lie back and float. Look up at the blue of the sky. It's crystal clear and breezy. Feel the warm breeze blow over you. Feel the softness of the cloud under you. Now just float and enjoy the softness and freedom."

2. Say, "Open your eyes. Today we're going to talk about our personal visions." Explain that you will focus on a special goal each person has of something he or she wants to achieve in life.

3. Read the quote by Wilma Rudolph on winning. Explain that Wilma Rudolph had a dream of winning a race, and that dream began when she was unable to walk. Explain that winning doesn't necessarily mean beating

someone else. People can win at life without having to defeat anyone.

4. Read "The Dream of Winning" (see Page 90). Discuss.

5. Ask the students what dreams or visions they have had for themselves. Tell them it's fine to have whatever positive visions they want, that nothing is too unrealistic to envision achieving. Say, "When Wilma Rudolph created her vision of running a race and winning, she couldn't even walk. It was her dream that gave her the strength and hope to move forward. What is your personal vision?"

6. Have the children close their eyes and picture their visions. Keep reiterating that no vision is too outrageous. Say, "Some of the most wonderful inventions and achievements in the world emerged from outrageous visions."

7. Give the students several minutes to

"image." Guide the children by asking: "What are you doing in your vision? How are you dressed? Are you with people or alone? How does it feel to be in your vision right now?"

8. Have students open their eyes and take turns sharing by going around the circle. Tape record each child. Affirm each vision by thanking every child who shares.

9. Pass out cloud patterns (on Page 92 for re-production) and paper, or blank papers for freehand drawing. Have the students create their visions in the cloud. When completed the children can paste cotton around the edges. Play back the tape.

10. Put the "Our Visions are Special" pictures on the bulletin board.

11. Have the children discuss their visions in small groups.

12. The children can do a journal entry: "My Personal Vision." Older children can write about their visions. Younger children can draw, this time about a different vision than what was expressed on the cloud.

THE DREAM OF WINNING

Wilma Rudolph (1940-   )*

Can you imagine what it would be like to lose your ability to walk? That's what happened to champion Wilma Rudolph when she was 4 years old. She got pneumonia, scarlet fever and then polio at the same time. She was very sick. She nearly died. Her left leg became so weak that she couldn't walk. Some kids would cry and pout if they couldn't walk. Not Wilma. Even though she was forced to sit in a chair, she still tried to play games with all her friends. Wilma had hope, and that kept her going. She was determined that one day, somehow, she would walk again.

Fortunately for Wilma, her family loved her very much. Both her parents worked full-time with only one day off each week. On that day Wilma's mother would drive her to the doctor in Nashville, Tennessee, 45 miles away. The doctor would massage Wilma's leg, to make it grow stronger.

Wilma had 22 brothers and sisters! Her mother taught 3 of them how to massage Wilma's leg. They massaged it 4 times a day.

Very slowly Wilma became stronger. When she was 6, she got a pair of special shoes. She could stand up and hop around on one leg. Finally, at the age of 11, Wilma was able to walk and run on her own, without any special shoes. Her hope had gotten her through!

Once she was able to move on her own, Wilma just couldn't be stopped. She started playing basketball. She soon made the school team. She was tall and thin. She could race down the court and shoot baskets better than anyone else. In her sophomore year, she scored 803 points in 25 games! It was an astonishing feat.

Wilma was even more astonishing when she took to track. She had a way of running that was pure poetry. Someone described it as "loose and sweet." Her body seemed to flow. Her arms pumped in rhythm. She seemed to run faster than any woman alive.

Wilma wanted to prove she was the best. At the age of 16 she entered the Olympics. Her relay team won a third place bronze medal. But when she ran by herself in the 200-meter dash, she didn't do well at all.

Wilma spent the next 4 years training. Every day she forced herself to run and run and then run some more.

When the 1960 Olympics arrived, Wilma was ready. She entered all the track events. She ended up winning 3 gold medals, a new record! Her team took first place in the 400-meter relay. By herself, she won the 100-meter dash and the 200-meter dash.

The world fell in love with Wilma. In Russia, people called her "Queen of the Olympics." In France, she was called "The Gazelle." And in Italy, they named her "The Black Pearl."

Just 16 years before, the fastest woman on earth had been unable to walk. The world will never forget the triumph of Wilma Rudolph.

Today Wilma Rudolph is head of the Wilma Rudolph Foundation. The purpose of the foundation is to help young people dream and achieve in the field of sports competition, as well as build character and self-image.

*Reprinted with permission, 1984 *Crayola Dream-makers Program,* Binney & Smith, Inc.

QUESTIONS TO DISCUSS

• What obstacles did Wilma Rudolph have to overcome?

• How did the dream of winning help Wilma to overcome those obstacles?

Here are some other people who dreamed of winning at sports. You might want to read their stories, too.

Babe Ruth

Jackie Robinson

Jim Thorpe

Pele

Althea Gibson

Babe Didrikson Zaharias

Bulletin Board 4
Learning the Skills of Peacemaking

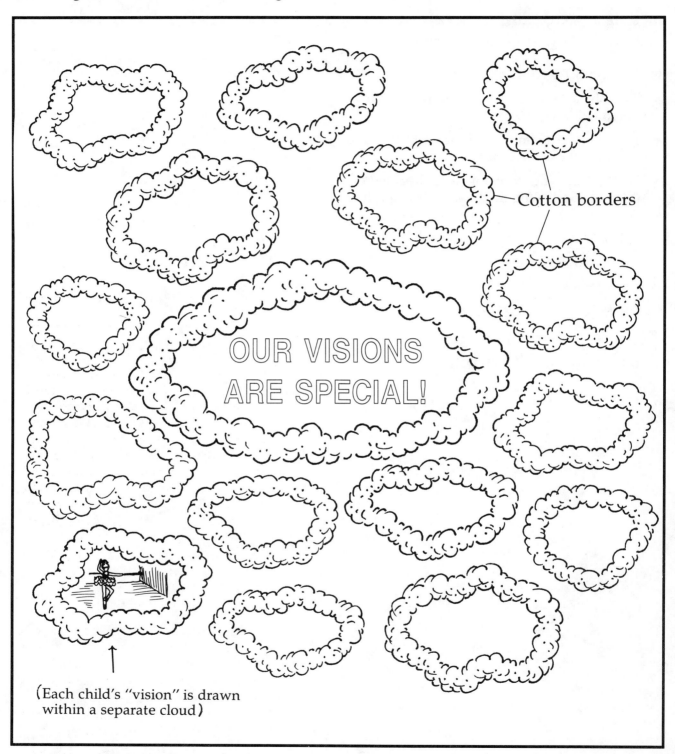

Cotton borders

OUR VISIONS
ARE SPECIAL!

(Each child's "vision" is drawn
within a separate cloud)

OUR VISION OF A PEACEFUL SCHOOL

OBJECTIVES

- The children will envision what their school would be like if it were totally peaceful.

- The children will draw distinctions between qualities of a peaceful and non-peaceful school.

- The children will collaborate on group murals of a "peaceful school."

   NOTE: This lesson correlates with Bulletin Board 5 entitled: "A Peaceful School Looks Like This."

MATERIALS

- Two pieces of poster paper with the headings:

   "A Non-Peaceful School"

   "A Peaceful School"

- Large sheets of mural paper—one for every group of five children

- Markers, crayons, any other art materials that can be used in creating a mural

- Journals

PROCEDURE

1. Have the children sit in a circle. State, "We have talked about how peace starts with us, and we've talked about our visions. Today we're going to combine these ideas and envision what it would be like to have a school that's totally peaceful, and the part we can play in making it that way."

2. Say, "The first thing I'm going to ask you to think about is the opposite of a peaceful school." Direct your class's attention to the poster, "A Non-Peaceful School." Ask your students to think for a moment of the way their school or any other school is when it's not peaceful. Say, "How do the people in the school treat each other in a non-peaceful setting? How does it feel?"

3. List the qualities of a non-peaceful school on the poster and discuss them.

4. Say, "Now we're going to do a process in which we will envision a school that is perfectly peaceful. The school you envision will be exactly the way you want it to be. No vision is too outrageous, so please don't limit your thoughts or judge them. Often the most creative ideas come out of thoughts we label as 'silly' or 'unrealistic.' The opportunity today is to allow yourself the freedom to envision whatever you choose." Allow time for questions

and brief discussion.

5. State, "Close your eyes and imagine our school being completely empty. Let's pretend it's the middle of the summer and nobody is here. There's nothing on the walls or bulletin boards. Everything is quiet and empty. There isn't even any furniture. Imagine you have all the money and help you need to decorate and furnish the school exactly as you'd like it to be. You might even want to take down some walls, or build an addition, or make the playground larger and add more to it.

   Imagine what your school would look like if you could have it exactly the very way you want it to be." Give the class a minute of complete silence in which to do this.

6. Say, "Now, picture people coming into your peaceful school. How do their faces look? How are they treating each other? Listen to their voices. How do they sound? What's it like in the halls and lunchroom and on the playground? Picture your teacher. How are he/she and the children relating to one another?"

7. Ask, "Are there any other people around? Adults? Parents? Are there any pets or animals? How do you feel in this school?" Give the children another minute or two to envision. Say, "Open your eyes."

8. Ask, "What was your vision like?" Discuss. Encourage the students to describe the different aspects of their visions. List portions of their descriptions on the poster entitled: "A Peaceful School."

9. After discussion have the class break up into teams of five. Give each team the large mural paper, markers, and crayons.

10. Say, "We're going to combine our individual visions into group visions. Take a few minutes to plan the creation of a mural of a peaceful school and its surrounding area. Decide who will draw the different parts. You'll be sharing the crayons and drawing materials together in each group. If you have a conflict, use the Win/Win Guidelines to work it out. Your job is to develop and complete your murals cooperatively in about twenty minutes. Any questions?"

11. Have students work in groups as you circulate. Note the processes they use to determine the content and development of their mural. Be available to help them mediate differences, but don't have them lean on you too heavily.

12. At the end of the lesson, have each group describe their mural to the class. Ask them also to describe the process they used to determine how the mural would be done. Ask if there were any conflicts and how they were handled.

13. State, "A peaceful world is dependent on people like you working together on many different projects. How can we as individuals take responsibility for working well together?" Discuss. "How can we as individuals have our school become the peaceful place we envision?" Guide your students to take on specific responsibilities in this regard. For example, children might state, "I'll work out my conflicts rather than fighting." or "I'll pick up litter in and around the school," or "If someone new comes to our school, I'll make friends with them so they're not alone."

Bulletin Board 5
Learning the Skills of Peacemaking

A PEACEFUL SCHOOL LOOKS LIKE THIS...

Children's "Group Mural"

Paper border

ALL GRADES

THE NICEST THING ABOUT...

OBJECTIVES

- The children will appreciate the special goodness in others.

- The children will observe, compare, and evaluate the positive qualities in their classmates.

    NOTE: This lesson correlates with Bulletin Board 6 entitled, "The Nicest Thing About ...."

MATERIALS

- 3 X 5 index cards

- Paper, crayons or magic markers

- Large face cut out

- Yarn (different colors), one for each child

- 4 X 6 white or manila paper

- scissors

PROCEDURE

1. Say, "Remember how we discussed peace starting with each individual. Remember how we as individuals created our visions of a peaceful school. Part of being peaceful is accepting and affirming one another. In today's lesson we're going to choose one person in our class we will affirm in a very special way."

2. Discuss with the children how each child has a special kind of goodness inside.

3. Choose one child to come forward.

    NOTE: This lesson is to be repeated every week or so until every child in the class has had a chance to be the focus.

4. Distribute the 3 X 5 file cards to every member of the class. Have each child write the name of the person you just selected on the top of the card. Their own name goes at the bottom.

5. Tell the children that the cards will be used after our discussion when each person can write one special quality on the card about the person in front of the room. Tell the children that the cards will go on the bulletin board entitled, "The Nicest Thing About . . ."

6. Ask the class to tell you what the special qualities are about the person selected. Discuss.

7. After the discussion is complete, have each child write on the 3 X 5 card a sentence expressing something about the special quality of the child in front of the room. For example, "Kenny is funny and he tells good jokes and

makes me laugh." Next, have each child draw and cut out a picture of his/her own face on the 4 X 6 paper.

    NOTE: For young children you will need an aide or helper to complete this part of the lesson.

8. While the class is working, give the large face cut-out to the selected child. Have the child draw his/her own face and hair on the cut-out.

9. Put the large face on the bulletin board. Hang each note card and small 4 X 6 picture around the face. Connect the yarn from each note card to the large face.

10. If you have access to a camera, take a picture of this bulletin board and send it home with the selected child.

Bulletin Board 6
Learning the Skills of Peacemaking

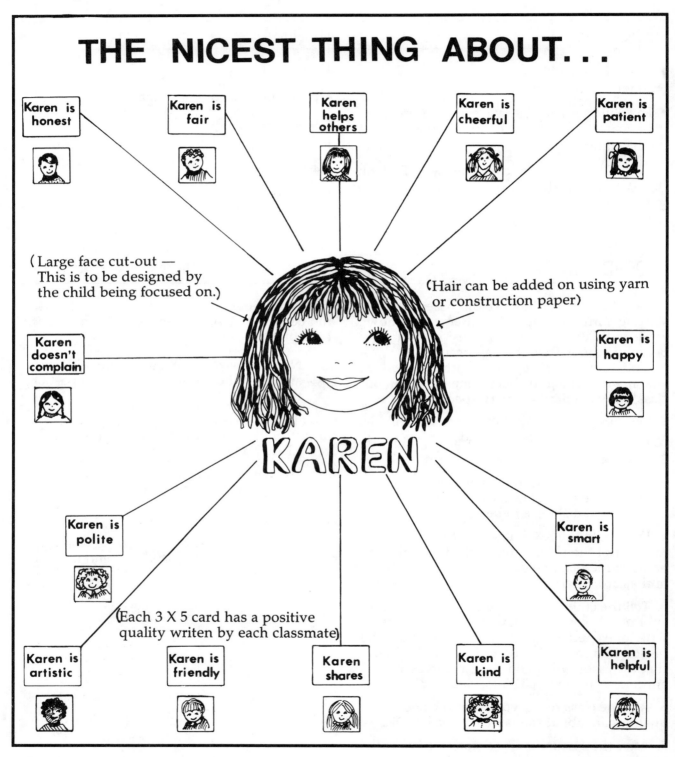

THE NICEST THING ABOUT...

Karen is honest

Karen is fair

Karen helps others

Karen is cheerful

Karen is patient

(Large face cut-out —
This is to be designed by
the child being focused on.)

(Hair can be added on using yarn
or construction paper)

Karen doesn't complain

Karen is happy

KAREN

Karen is polite

Karen is smart

(Each 3 X 5 card has a positive
quality writen by each classmate)

Karen is artistic

Karen is friendly

Karen shares

Karen is kind

Karen is helpful

BEING DIFFERENT IS OK

OBJECTIVES

- The children will develop a deeper understanding that all people have ways they are different from one another, but each individual is unique and special.

- The children will learn the value of being different.

- The children will develop a deeper understanding of the importance of accepting differences in others.

MATERIALS

- Poster with the following quote:

> "It has often proved true that the dream of yesterday is the hope of today and the reality of tomorrow."
> Robert Hutchings Goddard

- "The Dream of Unknown Worlds," Robert Hutchings Goddard (see Page 100)

- Diorama materials: shoe boxes, paste, scissors, crayons, pipe cleaners, clay, clothespins, etc.

PROCEDURE

1. Say, "Before we begin today's lesson we're going to do a new relaxation exercise. Close your eyes and picture yourself being able to fly. Spread your wings like a bird or butterfly and feel yourself gently lifting off the ground. Your body feels almost weightless as you float upward. Move your arms a little and propel yourself higher. Feel the air all around and under you. Nothing is holding you up, yet you won't fall down. Now look down beneath you. You see people and trees and flowers and buildings and animals. They all look small because you're up high. Yet you're perfectly safe because you can fly." Now have the children listen to the quietness in the classroom and feel the calmness within themselves. Ask them to open their eyes.

2. Say, "Everything of value that has ever been created by human beings has come from somebody's dream or vision. It is possible for us to make our vision become a reality." Discuss this concept and allow for questions. Say, "Now I'm going to read a very special quote from a very special person named Robert Goddard, whose vision has changed all of our lives." Read the quote on the poster: "It has often proved true that the dream of yesterday is the hope of

today, and the reality of tomorrow." Explain this thoroughly to the children, and make sure they understand it before going on.

3. Tell the children that you're going to read them a story about Robert Goddard and his special vision, but first go over the following points:

   a. We all have visions.

   b. Our visions are special.

   c. Nothing is too outrageous to envision.

   d. All of the wonderful achievements in the world have sprung from the visions of people like us.

4. Say, "I'm going to read you the story of Robert Hutchings Goddard who had a vision people considered to be so outrageous that they called him the "Moon Man," but that didn't stop him from making his vision a reality."

5. Read the text on Page 100, "The Dream of Unknown Worlds," and discuss it.

6. Ask the children, "Do you ever feel different? How?" Discuss, and as you listen, keep reinforcing that each child is special, and that it's fine to be different. Also reinforce that it's

important to accept differences in others, and that part of peacemaking is the acceptance of differences.

7. Ask, "How would our world be different today if Robert Goddard had given up his dream when people made fun of him?" Discuss. Keep reinforcing Goddard's courage and the importance of his vision and his willingness to take a stand in the face of obstacles. Discuss taking a stand. Tell the children what that means to you. Ask what it means to them.

8. Ask, "Have you ever given up a vision because of what other people have said?" This is a good time to share a personal anecdote about a vision or dream you gave up because of someone else's attitude or negative response.

9. Ask, "How can we encourage one another's visions?" Stress the value of acceptance, support, and caring for others.

10. Say, "Many of us have visions of making the world a better place. What is your vision of making the world a better place? What types of changes would you make?" Share your vision first. Have the children discuss ways in which they envision making the world a better place.

11. Have the children make dioramas entitled: "My Vision of Making the World a Better Place." This can be done at home or in school using shoe boxes or gift-sized boxes and mixed-media materials (fabric, pipe-cleaners, clay, magazine pictures, clothespins, paste, crayons, etc.)

12. Follow-up: When the dioramas are complete, have each child discuss their diorama and the vision it expresses. Dioramas can be displayed in the school library or another visible place in the school. Invite another class to see the dioramas and hear about the visions which inspired them.

THE DREAM OF UNKNOWN WORLDS

Robert Hutchings Goddard (1882-1945)*

People teased young Robert Goddard about being weird: he was really crazy about machines. As soon as he could talk, he started asking scientific questions. He tried experiments, too. Once he made a balloon with helium, but it failed to rise off the ground.

Robert was always daydreaming about faraway places and unknown worlds. His favorite story was The War of the Worlds about an invasion from Mars.

One of Robert's own daydreams was so vivid that it seemed real to him. It happened when he was 17 years old. He was climbing a cherry tree in his grandmother's orchard to prune a dead limb. He looked into the sky. Suddenly he imagined he was in a flying machine. The machine had some sort of device that allowed it to escape the pull of gravity and soar off into space. Robert felt as if he were flying to the moon!

Robert spent the rest of his life trying to make this daydream come true. First he studied physics, the science of energy and motion. Then he started building his own rockets and shooting them off. The launching began to attract attention. People thought Goddard was crazy. The newspapers called him the "Moon Man." His home state of Massachusetts even banned his launchings there, for fear they would cause brush fires!

Goddard had other problems, too. He was often sick. His body was thin and frail. For most of his life he suffered from tuberculosis. But Goddard didn't give up. He finally found a few other people who believed in his dream and that helped him to continue his experiments.

Many of his experiments were failures. He never came close to getting a rocket to the moon. The moon is 240,000 miles away. Goddard's greatest rocket went only 9,000 feet up — not quite two miles. Nevertheless, Robert Goddard is known as the father of modern rocketry. He took out patents for 200 rocketry inventions. Two of his discoveries were especially important. There is hardly any air in outer space: it is nearly a vacuum. Goddard was the first to prove that a rocket could fly within a vacuum. He also discovered the first solid rocket fuel which makes today's space travel possible.

When Goddard died in 1945, he still believed

in his dream of unknown worlds. He was sure that people would fly to the moon.

*Reprinted with permission, 1984 *Crayola Dream-maker Program*, Binney & Smith, Inc.

QUESTIONS TO DISCUSS

- Did Goddard's dream ever come true?
- Who made it come true? When did it happen?

Here are some people who dreamed of unknown worlds:

Marco Polo

Christopher Columbus

Lewis, Clark, and Sacagawea.

You might want to read their stories, too.

OTHER PEOPLE ARE DIFFERENT TOO

OBJECTIVES

- The children will explore attitudes toward differences in others.

- The children will pinpoint specific differences to which they have reacted in the past (racial, gender, ethnic, age, handicap, religious, other).

- The children will learn that as peacemakers they need to accept the differences in others.

- The children will collaborate on a group mural.

    NOTE: This lesson correlates with Bulletin Board 7 entitled "We Celebrate Our Differences."

MATERIALS

- Poem: "Kids Are Different" (see Page 105)

- National Geographic or another magazine which has pictures of people of different races, colors, ethnic origins, ages, genders. Pictures of handicapped people are very appropriate also. These magazines will be used for cutting up.

- Paste, scissors

- Large mural paper with heading: "We Celebrate Our Differences" The paper should be large enough for each child in the class to paste several pictures on. Make sure the mural paper will fit on your bulletin board.

PROCEDURE

1. Have the children sit in a circle. Do a brief relaxation exercise and read the poem, "Kids Are Different." Discuss the concept of human differences. Ask what kinds of human differences were referred to in the poem. Ask, "How do you feel when you're with people who are different from you?" Discuss. Ask, "Is it okay for people to be different, or would it be better if we were all the same?" Discuss. On the board, write the terms: ethnic, racial, gender, handicap, religion. Describe the meaning of each term and ask the children how people seem to react to these differences in others. Discuss.

2. Have each of the children turn to the person they are sitting next to.

3. Say, "Look at your partner. How is he/she different from you?" Discuss this together. Acknowledge each person who speaks.

4. Ask, "What differences did you notice in your partner?" Discuss and keep reiterating that we all differ from one another in many ways. Acknowledge each person who speaks.

5. Ask, "Have you ever seen or known

someone who was different than you? How did those differences make you feel?" Discuss and stress that it is okay to have feelings, whatever they may be. Ultimately it is our actions that make a difference. Children may feel awkward or guilty about being put off by differences. Let them know that they are not alone in feeling this way, but that the process of learning to value each individual as special and unique is an important one.

6. Say, "We are all different in some way. How does it make you feel when someone puts you down for being different?"

7. Ask, "If we want to create a peaceful world, how can we treat people who we perceive as being different? Remember, we are all different in some way. How are you different?" Discuss. Guide the students to understand the value of taking responsibility for their actions and attitudes, as well as the importance of accepting others.

8. Say, "If we want a world at peace, then we must start, as individuals, with an attitude of acceptance and understanding. Can we expect nations of the world to accept one another's

differences if we cannot be accepting as individuals?" Discuss. Reiterate that we are all the same inside.

9. Reiterate that peace starts with the individual.

10. Have your students work in small groups, locating and cutting out pictures of people of different colors, races, ages, genders, etc. Encourage your students to discuss the concept of acceptance of human differences as they work.

11. Remind your students that this is a collaborative activity. Explain the meaning of the word collaborative. State, "If we're each going to take full responsibility for having the kind of world we want, then we must find ways to work collaboratively in large and small groups.

12. Direct attention to the mural paper entitled, "We Celebrate Our Differences." Have the class paste their pictures on the mural paper. Encourage them to work out ways to take turns and not get in each other's way. Note the process the children use to do this, and discuss the process with them. Note what works and what doesn't work. Discuss.

13. Conclude by guiding the students to reiterate the value of being different and accepting differences in others. Finally, stress again that peace starts with the individual and that each person's actions make an impact on the world.

KIDS ARE DIFFERENT

Kids are diff'rent
We don't even look the same
Some kids speak diff'rent languages
We all have a different name
Kids are different
But if you look inside you'll see
That tall kid, that small kid
Is just like you and me.
Some folks are surprised that
Kids in wheelchairs play
Blind kids read, deaf kids talk
Except in a diff'rent way.
Able kids, disabled kids
There's nothing we can't do
Just take a look inside yourself
You'll be so proud of you
Because
Kids are diff'rent
We don't even look the same
Some kids speak diff'rent languages
We all have a different name.
Kids are diff'rent
But if you look inside you'll see
That tall kid, that small kid
That deaf kid, that blind kid
Are just like you and me.

From *"Kids on the Block."*
Lyrics, Barbara Aiello; Music, Bud Forrest. Permission to reprint granted to all who wish to reproduce the words to this song.

Bulletin Board 7
Learning the Skills of Peacemaking

WE CELEBRATE OUR DIFFERENCES!

Collage of magazine pictures indicating human differences

(Paper border)

OUR FEELINGS ARE OK

OBJECTIVES

- The children will learn that people all have a variety of different feelings.

- The children will understand that it's important to accept their own feelings and the feelings of others.

- The children will understand that human beings must be responsible for "owning" their feelings and actions, and that they can choose their actions.

- The children will practice using "I messages."

MATERIALS

- Optional: From the book *Free To Be You and Me* — The story, "It's Alright To Cry"

- Pictures of people showing emotion (happiness, sadness, anger, surprise, fear). You can have the children bring these in ahead of time.

- Large mural paper entitled: "All Kinds of Feelings"

- Markers (for grades 2-6)

- Large poster with the words: Accept Your Feelings, and Choose Your Actions Wisely.

PROCEDURE

1. Have the children form a circle. If you have the book, *Free To Be You And Me,* read the story "It's Alright To Cry." Discuss the feelings of sadness expressed by the main character. This is optional. If you do not have the book, ask students to share about a time they've felt sad about something. Have several people share.

2. Ask the students to share the way they feel right now. Accept any answer. Encourage full participation.

3. Show pictures of people with different feelings. Discuss.

4. Show the children the mural paper entitled: "All Kinds of Feelings." Ask them to tell you about the different feelings they have experienced. Place the paper on the floor and give each child a marker. Ask the students to write down any feeling they have ever had. Give them five to ten minutes. Younger children can illustrate the feelings using pictures of facial expressions.

5. After the time has elapsed, have the children form a circle. Tell them, "Feelings are a natural part of who we are." Refer to the poster: "Accept Your Feelings, and Choose Your Actions Wisely." Say, "What does this mean?"

Discuss. Stress the concept that people can choose how they want to act. Example: "Just because someone is angry, that person doesn't have to hit. He or she can choose to express feelings in another way."

6. State, "Part of being a responsible member of the human family is realizing that we are the owners of our feelings. No one else can put feelings inside us. Other people can trigger our feelings, but ultimately the feelings are our own."

7. Say, "Each of us is whole and special and wonderful, even when we are angry or resentful. We don't become the feelings we are experiencing. When we feel angry, we are not bad, just angry. We must remember above all that we decide how we're going to act, and we must choose our actions carefully, always considering the feelings of others." Discuss alternatives for the expression of anger. Say, "What are some of the things you can do when you're angry so you don't hurt anyone?"

8. Hang up the poster "Accept Your Feelings" in the front of the room. Group the children into pairs. Ask each pair to complete these

sentences, taking turns:

I feel happy when _____

I feel sad when _____

I feel angry when _____

I feel scared when _____

I feel great when _____

Discuss.

9. Say, "When we have conflicts with other people, lots of different feelings can surface. You may feel angry, frightened, frustrated, or sad." Give a personal example. Ask, "Have any of you had any recent conflicts you would like to share?" Ask the children to describe how they felt during the conflict.

10. Choose a conflict to have children act out. Ask for volunteers to play the parts of the various "characters," but don't use real names. Review the Win/Win Guidelines.

11. Have the volunteers role play a conflict in the center of the room. Coach them in stating feelings with "I messages."

12. When the role play is complete, ask, "Do you think the things you're learning about feelings and conflicts can help you get along with others?" Discuss.

13. Stress that each time the children choose to work out their differences non-violently, they are helping to make the world more peaceful. Say, "Imagine what it would be like if everyone resolved their conflicts without the use of violence. What would the world be like?" Have the children share their responses.

MY FRIEND IS DIFFERENT AND HE/SHE IS SPECIAL

OBJECTIVES

- The children will understand that human differences make people unique and special.
- The children will reiterate the need for accepting others and valuing their uniqueness.
- The children will begin booklets entitled, "My Friend Is Different and He/She Is Special."

MATERIALS

- Large poster entitled

> "ABOUT HUMAN DIFFERENCES"
> 1. Human beings are different in many ways, but we're all the same inside.
> 2. All people have the same basic needs: food, clothing, shelter, and love.
> 3. Our differences make us special and unique.
> 4. Peacemaking means accepting ourselves and others.
> 5. Affirming others for their uniqueness is important.
> 6. We all are interconnected regardless of our differences.

- Construction paper (9 X 12) for front/back cover of booklets
- Five or more pieces of drawing or writing paper per child (or five "My Friend Is Different and He/She Is Special" booklets—see Page 111)
- Crayons, pencils, markers
- Chart entitled: "Human Beings Are Different and Special in Many Ways"

PROCEDURE

1. Have the children sit in a circle. Ask, "What did you learn about human differences in other lessons we have done?"

2. Show the poster "About Human Differences" and discuss the concepts. Guide the children to restate the concepts on the chart, in their own words, by asking what each sentence means.

3. Say, "Think about your friends. Think about how they are different from you. Close your eyes. Picture your best friend. What is different about him or her? What is special?" Discuss.

4. Have the children turn to the person they're sitting next to for paired sharing.

5. Say, "We're going to take a few moments to

tell our partners about a friend we have who is both different and special." You can start with an example of someone in your own life; for example, you could say, 'My friend uses a cane to walk. Sometimes it's hard for her to get around. My friend is also very special because she's kind and she's smart.'" Give the class about four minutes to share in pairs.

6. Distribute papers for booklets. Younger children can illustrate the contents of the booklet. Older children can draw and write. Say, "We're going to think of five people we know who are different and special. On each page you will draw/write what's different about them and what's special." [You can reproduce the text on Page 111 for student booklets.] Again, stress the value of accepting human differences and the fact that we're all the same inside.

7. Follow-up: Have each child share his/her booklet with the class, describing the friends they wrote and drew about.

> NOTE: The booklet can be completed at home, rather than in class. Be sure to have the children present their booklets to one another as oral reports when they are finished. This will be a great time to invite the parents in.

MY FRIEND IS DIFFERENT AND HE/SHE IS SPECIAL

Name:

Date:

Directions: Choose five people. On each page, write their first name and fill out the following:

My friend's name is:

He/She is different because:

He/She is special because:

Draw a picture of your special friend.

HUMAN DIFFERENCES: BEING JAIME

OBJECTIVES

- The children will put themselves in the place of someone who is "the different one."
- The children will develop an understanding of other people's reactions to differences.
- The children will develop an understanding of what it would be like to be the object of prejudice.

MATERIALS

- Poster: "About Human Differences"
- Drawing paper, crayons, or markers
- Journals

PROCEDURE

NOTE: Be sure to exercise extreme sensitivity in doing this lesson. Read "Being Jaime" to yourself first (below). If there are children in your class whose lives resemble Jaime's, decide ahead of time how to handle the presentation of the lesson.

1. Have the children form a circle. Review the poster from Lesson 31, "About Human Differences." Say, "We have discussed differences and what it is like to be the different one. Today we are going to imagine what it would be like to be a child named Jaime who is different than many of the other children in the school. As I read the story about Jaime I want you to imagine that you are Jaime. Jaime can be either a boy or a girl."

BEING JAIME

Jaime is nine years old. Jaime and his/her mother live with an aunt in a tiny apartment over an old hardware store. Jaime's mother cleans other people's homes for a living. She has very little money to buy clothes for Jaime, so Jaime has to wear old hand-me-downs. Jaime goes to school in a neighborhood where all the other children have nice clothes and live in big houses with pretty lawns. Imagine that you are Jaime. What would your life be like? How is Jaime's life like yours? How is it different?

2. Say, "Now close your eyes and continue to imagine yourselves as Jaime. Picture yourself living with your mother and aunt in the tiny apartment above the hardware store. You have very few toys and the television is broken. Mom doesn't make enough money to get it fixed. You are cold because there has been no heat in your apartment this week. It's time for school. You put on your best outfit, but there is a rip in the sleeve. Your sneakers are old and the laces are broken and knotted in different places. You go outside to walk to school. You see other children walking in small groups, laughing and talking together. How do they act when they see you? What do they say? How do you feel? You get to school and go inside. The children continue to talk and laugh. They discuss the shows they watched on television last night. You walk through the crowd of children and go to your seat in the back of the room. You wait for the teacher to take attendance. How do the other children look at you? What do they say? How do you feel? What do you want to do? What do you wish the other children would do?" Allow a few moments of silence, eyes closed.

3. Say, "Open your eyes. How did you feel being Jaime?" Discuss.

4. Ask, "How would your life be different from the way it is now if you were Jaime? Have you ever known anyone like Jaime? Have you ever felt like Jaime might feel?" Give the children ample time to discuss.

5. Say, "If we want to have a world in which people accept and cooperate with one another, how should we treat people who appear to be different than we are?"

6. State, "Remember, we always have a choice. As human beings, it is our responsibility to choose our actions carefully and appropriately. How can the actions chosen by the children around Jaime make Jaime's life a happier one?"

7. State, "Are you willing to make a commitment to being accepting of others?" Review the meaning of the word commitment.

8. Say, "Imagine the different countries of the world treating each other with acceptance rather than non-acceptance. How would the world be different than it is now?"

9. Ask the children to draw Jaime's picture as he/she goes to school or is in class with the other children.

10. Have older children write in their journals about what it was like to be Jaime. Younger children can use drawing paper and crayons or markers to express their feelings.

DIFFERENT FLAGS OF DIFFERENT LANDS

OBJECTIVES

- The children will learn about different countries of the world through the use of pictures of flags.

- Each child will draw a flag of a different country.

- The children will begin research projects on the country associated with their flag.

MATERIALS

- Encyclopedias or dictionaries with pictures of flags; try to gather extras because the children will be copying the flags

- Names of different countries printed on small squares of paper or note cards to be picked out of a box (have one country for each child)

- World map or globe

- Research project contracts (see Page 118)

- Note to parents (see Page 117)

- Construction paper, crayons, rulers, paint (optional), scissors, and paste

  NOTE: You may want to make special arrangements with your school librarian before starting this project. It would be best to do a portion of this lesson in the library, so that each child can make a rough draft of his/her flag using books available there. It would also be helpful to have posted a chart with each child's name, country, and the due date of the project. You may want to give a brief overview of map skills before this lesson. The children will be locating various countries on the map or globe during the lesson.

PROCEDURE

1. Have the children form a circle. Say, "We know that our world is made up of many different kinds of people. Our differences make the world a more diverse (explain) and interesting place to live. We've talked about accepting differences. Sometimes it's easier to do this when we know more about the culture and background of other people. Today we're going to begin a project which will help us do just that." Show the encyclopedia or dictionary pages containing the flags of the world. Say: "Members of the human family come from many different countries throughout the world.

We are all part of one world, one earth. These flags represent the different places in which the people of the world live."

2. Say, "Today we are each going to make a flag and choose a country to do a project on."

3. Say, "We're going to play a game called 'Pick a Country.'" Ask each child to close his/her eyes and pick the name of a country from a box. Have each child locate the country on the map or globe. Help the children find the country they are looking for. (For remote countries, list the continent along with the country on each

paper you place in the box.)

4. After each child has found the country, say, "We are going to begin research projects about our different countries." Explain the meaning of the words research project.

5. Hand out the research project contracts. Go over them. Explain to the students that they can work with their parents on this project if they need help. Show them the letters for their parents.

6. Have the children fill in the blanks of both the contract and the letter.

7. Explain that the projects will help everyone learn more about the world in which they live. Say, "We will be finding out about other people with whom we share our planet."

> NOTE: The portion of the lesson that can be done in the library follows.

8. Say, "Let's begin by making a practice drawing of the flag of each of our countries." Distribute the dictionaries and encyclopedias and have the children do their practice copies. Tell the children they will make a larger flag with construction paper, paste, crayons, and markers. Say, "Draw and color carefully so that you can use your picture as a model."

9. If there is enough time, have the children make their larger flag the same day. If not, this part of the lesson can be done the following day.

10. Say, "Remember, we are all interconnected; we are connected to all the other people on earth as a human family." Reiterate how their projects will help the students learn about people with whom they share the earth.

NOTE TO PARENTS
Learning the Skills of Peacemaking
Lesson 33

Dear Parents:

As part of Learning the Skills of Peacemaking, your child has brought home a picture a flag he/she has created from _____. He/she has been asked to

country

complete a research project on that country. Would you assist your child in finding the following information:

1. location of country
2. map of country (student draws this)
3. population
4. traditional foods
5. most common jobs
6. native dwelling (describe, draw, or make model of, if available)
7. other interesting facts

Your child should write, in his/her own words, a report on his/her country including the above information. Although this project should be done by your child, your assistance and guidance will be most helpful. Please contact me if there are any questions. I would be happy to discuss them with you.

Sincerely,

Teacher's Name_____

Due Date_____

Student's Name_____

- Tear Off and Return -

I _____ agree to help my child _____
  (Parent)   (Name)

complete his/her research project by _____
                                                  (Date)

Signature _____

RESEARCH PROJECT CONTRACT
Learning the Skills of Peacemaking
Lesson 33

"I, _____ agree to be responsible for the
(Student's name)

completion of my research project on _____ by
(Country)

_____ .
(Due date)

I agree to get the help I need in order to finish carefully and on time. I agree to meet with (my teacher) if I have a problem.

_____   _____

Signature of Student   Date

DIFFERENT FLAGS: ORAL REPORTS

OBJECTIVES

- The children will present their research projects orally.

- The children will each "become the teacher" during his/her presentation. They use map, globe, pointer, and any other visuals they request.

    NOTE: For this lesson, older children can make their own transparencies for their presentation and use the overhead projector. Students may also enjoy using the opaque projector. Encourage them to bring in any other visuals they might have or can create relating to their projects.

MATERIALS

- Research projects
- Maps, globes, pointer
- Projector (optional)
- Tape recorder to record each child's report (optional)
- Optional: a baked or cooked "treat" from the countries being reported on

PROCEDURE

1. Children present research projects, one at a time, in front of the class. They locate their country on the map or globe. Each child's flag should be displayed when they are giving their reports. Any other visuals should be shown at this time.

2. Discuss each report briefly. Encourage children to draw comparisons among the countries. Optional: Tape record each report. Children can listen to themselves with headphones during free time.

3. Display all reports and visuals.

4. Invite another class in to see the displayed reports and flags. Each child in your class can tell the other children what country they worked on.

TAKING PART IN OUR COMMUNITIES

OBJECTIVES

- The children will choose a community or school problem on which they would like to focus.

- The children will brainstorm solutions to this problem in small groups.

- The children will choose a solution and describe a plan of action.

  NOTE: First grade teachers will need the assistance of parents, aides, or several children from a higher grade to help record brainstorming ideas.

MATERIALS

- Brainstorming Poster from Lesson 10.

- Large Poster entitled: "Things Needing Improvement"

- One piece of chart paper and marker for each group

- Journals

PROCEDURE

1. Have the students form a circle. Tell them that this lesson will focus on thinking about solutions to community or school problems. Ask the class to choose whether they want to focus on the community or the school.

2. After the decision is made, ask the students to think of things they see in need of improvement or change. (For example, a school problem might be litter on the playground. A community problem might be the need for low-cost housing.)

3. Record suggested problem areas on the "Things Needing Improvement" poster.

4. After a sufficient amount of suggestions have been made, the class can vote on the problem which they would like to focus on.

5. Review the Brainstorming Poster thoroughly. Say, "Today we're going to use the process of brainstorming to come up with solutions to the problem we've just discussed."

6. Have the children break up into "problem-solving groups" of four or five. They pick a leader. Explain that the leader records the ideas of the group. Pass out the chart paper and markers. Say, "Take five to ten minutes and

brainstorm all the ideas you can. Remember, everybody has good ideas and everybody's ideas are worthwhile." (For young children, the helper will record.)

7. Allow the children five to ten minutes to brainstorm solutions.

8. Stop the discussion after ten minutes and ask the children to decide on one solution per group. This should take about five minutes. Remind them to use the Win/Win Guidelines when needed.

9. Ask the group leaders to share the solutions his/her group came up with. Then have the class vote on the best solution.

10. Once the solution has been agreed upon, say, "We now need to implement a plan of action." Talk about specific steps that can be taken to address the problem. For example, if the students focused on a school problem, they can write letters to the principal describing the problem and outlining their solutions. Or perhaps a group of students will visit the principal to discuss the class' concern about the problem, and to let him or her know of their suggested solution. For community problems, the class can write or phone the mayor or town

council, write a letter to the local newspaper, or come up with their own way of solving the problem.

11. Follow-up: Have students in grades 2-6 expand on this topic in their journals. The entry can be entitled "How I Can Make a Difference in My School or Community." The students can describe another problem they are aware of, listing possible solutions. They can come up with ideas about what kids can do to deal with the problem. (Younger students can illustrate the problem on one page and the solution on another in their journals.)

SENTENCE WRITING USING FAMILIAR TERMS

OBJECTIVES

- The children will discuss the meaning of new terms used in past lessons.

- The children will re-state the meaning of each term.

- The children will use these terms in a sentence, either oral or written, to show that they understand the meaning.

    NOTE: Teachers from Grade 1 who want to use this lesson can discuss and review the meaning of each term, rather than have the children write them. I was able to eventually have my first graders write sentences using the terms. In fact they loved the idea of using and understanding "grown-up" words. I laughed with one parent when she told me how her six-year-old came home and asked her to "affirm" him.

MATERIALS

- Large chart entitled: "Peacemaking Terms" (see Page 124)

- Paper and pencils

PROCEDURE

1. Have the children sit in a circle.

2. Direct their attention to the poster, "Peacemaking Terms." Go around circle and have the children talk about each term. Discuss the meanings together. Help the class clear up any misunderstandings they have about each term.

3. Divide the list of terms into groups of five or six words. On selected days have your students write the definitions of each term and then use each term in a sentence.

4. Have the children work as partners. Those who need extra assistance can work with others who have a better grasp of the meaning and use of each term. Stress the value of cooperation and helping one another.

PEACEMAKING TERMS

cooperate
conflict
resolution
affirm
acknowledge
peace
ethnic
racial
handicap
gender
unique
brainstorm
vision
reality
interconnected
I Message
Win/Win
well-being
peacemaker
contribution
problem-solving
commitment
considerate
responsibility

CONFLICTS IN THE NEWS

NOTE: Send home Current Events Letters to Parents from Lesson 24 ahead of time and before proceeding.

OBJECTIVES

NOTE: First grade teachers who do this lesson will need the assistance of parents, aides, or older children to record brainstorming solutions.

- The children will each bring in a current events article focusing on a conflict at any level (interpersonal, local, global).

- The children will use brainstorming to come up with solution for a conflict in the news.

- The children will understand that they have the ability to express themselves and "make a difference," regardless of their age.

    NOTE: This lesson correlates with Bulletin Board 8 entitled: "Problems in the News: Kids Have the Answers!"

MATERIALS

- Current events article about a conflict of some kind. (Each child should be asked to bring one in ahead of time.)
- Win/Win Guidelines
- Large chart paper and marker for each problem solving group of five students
- 5" X 7" piece of paper for each child to cut out into face shape and draw his/her face on.
- Crayons/markers to color face cut-outs
- Scissors

PROCEDURE

1. Have the children sit in a circle with their current events articles. Say, "Just as we have the ability to make a difference and express our opinions about school and community issues, we can also express ourselves about national and global issues, particularly in regard to issues appearing in the news.

2. Say, "Today we're going to examine some articles you have brought in from the newspapers or magazines. We're going to go around the circle and I'd like each person to tell in a few sentences what his or her article is about."

3. Have each child briefly describe his/her article and state the conflict represented within.

4. After each child has spoken, choose one article on which to focus. Read or paraphrase it for the class and then have the class restate the conflict situation. On the board, write a sentence expressing the conflict.

5. Direct the students' attention to the Win/Win Guidelines. Review them and ask the children to think about how the guidelines can be applied to the conflict in the article. Discuss.

6. Have the class divide into problem solving groups of four or five. Ask each group to choose a leader who will record the suggestions of his/her teammates on chart paper. (Here's where first graders will need the help of parents, aides, or older children. The leader can ask for ideas, and the helper will record.) Encourage the students to choose people who have not been a leader before.

7. Ask the children to think of the Win/Win Guidelines in discussing the conflict in the article. Ask them to give particular attention to "brainstorming" solutions. Remind them that no solution is too outrageous to state. Encourage them to be as creative as possible when brainstorming. Let them know that they will eventually choose only one or two solutions (perhaps combining several), and that the creative process will unlock new ideas.

8. Say, "I am going to give you seven to ten minutes to generate your ideas and decide on a solution." Distribute the chart paper and markers to each group. Be sure the Win/Win Guidelines are available for reference. Observe how the students apply the process, and be available to mediate differences. Encourage them to be sensitive to the feelings of people on both sides of the conflict represented in the article.

9. After the allotted time, have each group leader present the solution decided upon and comment on how the problem-solving process was used in the group.

10. Write the solution presented by each group on the board. Have the students vote on which solution they would like to support as a class.

11. Write a class letter to the newspaper or magazine from which the article was taken and outline the solution.

12. Distribute the 5" X 7" pieces of paper and have each child draw and color his/her face, and cut it out. Tell the children that their "faces" will go on the "Problems in the News: Kids Have the Answers" bulletin board.

13. During the month, be sure to look in the "Letters" section of the newspaper or magazine for your class's letter. When the letter is printed, copy it and give one to each member of the class to take home.

14. Be sure to hang the printed letter on the bulletin board. If the letter doesn't get in the paper, hang your own copy of it on the bulletin board. Stress to the class that their ideas make a difference. State, "No matter how young or old you are, you have the ability to make a difference in the world. You can express yourselves to the newspapers and elected officials on any issue you feel is important."

NOTE: A sample Letter to the Editor is presented below. The conflict addressed was the burning of a house owned by a black family in a white neighborhood and the desecration of a temple in the same neighborhood.

LETTER TO THE EDITOR

Dear Editor:

   Being kind to others is very important. We feel badly that a house was burnt down in the development near our school. We heard this happened because the family had a different color skin. We believe we should be kind to people of different colors and religions. We also feel bad that the temple has a hole in it. We think everybody should be kind to one another. We want to live in a peaceful world. This earth is a good place to be. Even if you're a German, Israeli, Indian, it doesn't matter where you come from. It does matter how you act. It doesn't matter where you come from or how you look. You are a part of this world. We're sorry that people got killed in wars. Please be kind to one another.

                              Sincerely,

                              Mrs. Drew's First Grade

NOTE: Be sure to include the name of every child in your class when you do this. This will be a priceless and long-remembered experience for all of them, and for those who read the letter.

Bulletin Board 8
Learning the Skills of Peacemaking

FINDING THE PEACEMAKERS

NOTE: Be sure to send home in advance the
Letter to Parents at the end of this lesson.

OBJECTIVES

- The children will describe the qualities of
  peacemakers in the articles, stories, and
  pictures they have brought in.

- The children will practice reflective listening.

- The children will collaboratively create
  pictures of peacemakers.

  NOTE: This lesson correlates with Bulletin
  Board 9 entitled "Peacemakers in Our
  World."

MATERIALS

- Letter to Parents to be given out prior to the
  lesson (see Page 130)

- Current events articles,
  books, and stories children have brought in
  describing peacemakers

- "A Peacemaker Is Someone Who" poster from
  Lesson 17

- Journals

PROCEDURE

1. Ask the children to bring their articles, books,
and stories on peacemakers to the circle.

2. Go over the "A Peacemaker Is Someone
Who. . ." poster.

3. Have each of the children turn toward the
person they are sitting next to for "paired
sharing."

4. Say, "Each of you is going to tell your
partner about the peacemaker in your article,
book, or story. We'll take about five minutes to
share, and then you will each tell the class
about your partner's peacemaker. Remember to
listen carefully while your partner speaks."

5. Give the class five to six minutes for paired
sharing.

6. Have each child tell briefly about his/her
partner's peacemaker.

7. Have the partners select together the most
interesting peacemaker they heard about today.

8. Ask the partners to draw a picture of that
peacemaker together. Allow the children to
figure out how they're going to do this. Each
pair of children should end up with one picture
on which they both worked.

9. Display the finished pictures on the bulletin
board.

10. Have the children write about the process
of working the picture together, and the
peacemaker they chose, in their journals.
(Younger children can do illustrations.)

LETTER TO PARENTS

Dear Parents,
Your children have been asked to locate articles and pictures of people who are peacemakers in newspapers, magazines, and books. Will you please assist them in finding what they need and in going over the content of the article or story about the peacemakers they have selected. As always, thank you for your willingness to help.

Sincerely,

_____
Teacher

_____
Date

Bulletin Board 9
Learning the Skills of Peacemaking

PEACEMAKERS IN OUR WORLD

George Washington

Martin Luther King

Ghandi

Mother Theresa

This bulletin board contains a combination of pictures and photos of peacemakers

Pictures can be hand-drawn and cut out. Captions should be placed beneath each picture.

BUILDING A "CIVILIZATION OF LOVE"

OBJECTIVES

- The children will define what a "Civilization of Love" means to them.

- The children will envision what a "Civilization of Love" would be like.

- The children will discuss the following concept: "respect for the unique dignity of each human being."

MATERIALS

- Large chart paper entitled: "A Civilization of Love"

- Mural paper entitled: "A Civilization of Love"

- Markers, paints, crayons, etc.

- Definitions on a poster for: unique, dignity, civilization and respect

- Books on Gandhi (optional)

PROCEDURE

1. Have the class form a circle. Do the following relaxation exercise. Say, "Close your eyes. Imagine yourself walking into a room filled with people you don't know, but you feel perfectly safe and relaxed. It is a bright sunny room. The people are smiling and talking quietly. They smile at you and immediately start talking to you, just as if they had always known you. You feel perfectly comfortable. You know that these people care about you, even though they didn't know you before. You notice that the people have skin of different colors and different facial characteristics. Some are black, some white, some Oriental, some Indian, some Hispanic. You begin to feel like they are your family. You feel safe, loved, and accepted in this room. You don't want to leave it. You know you are in a special place."

2. Have the children open their eyes and describe how they feel.

3. Tell them that you are now going to read them an excerpt from the newspaper of a statement by Pope John Paul. Let the class know that Pope John Paul is a peacemaker, and that in the article he talks about another famous peacemaker, perhaps the most famous one of all, Mahatma Gandhi.

4. Ask, "Who knows who Gandhi was and why people all over the world respect him so much?" Discuss and give some background on

Gandhi. If you have a book on Gandhi, show it now and display any photos.

5. Read the following newspaper excerpt once, then re-read it, making sure that your class understands what you're reading. Go over the definitions and give all of the explanation the children need. "Mahatma Gandhi taught that if all men and women, whatever the differences between them, cling to the truth, with respect for the unique dignity of every human being, a new world order — a civilization of love — can be achieved." (*The Star Ledger*, Newark, NJ; February 1, 1986)

6. Ask, "What would a 'civilization of love' be like?" Share your own feelings about this.

7. Go around the circle and have the children give their interpretations and feelings.

8. Ask, "What does 'respect for the unique dignity of each human being' mean?" Discuss.

9. Have the children close their eyes and envision, in silence, "a civilization of love where the unique dignity of every human being would be respected."

10. After about three minutes, have the children share their visions. Record the elements of the visions: feelings, descriptions, etc. on the chart paper.

11. Put the mural paper entitled: "A Civilization

of Love" on the floor. Move the desks. Pass out the paints, etc. Let the children spread out and compose a mural together as a whole class. They should take about five minutes ahead of time to plan how they will do this.

12. Stress that this is a collaborative effort in which they will demonstrate the principles of peace and cooperation to which Gandhi dedicated his life.

13. Follow-up: Invite the principal to see the mural. Create an opportunity to display it to the parents. Call the local newspapers and ask them to take a picture of it with the class. Let the children know that, through their artistic expressions, they are making a huge difference, and they are sending a message to all the people who see their mural.

MEASURING THE UNDERSTANDINGS LEARNED IN THIS GUIDE

STAGE II: Integrating Peacemaking Into Our Lives

NOTE: You can use this page as a test of the understandings in Stage II, with age groups where this is appropriate. You can also use the questions to orally survey your students to find out their depth of understanding of the concepts covered.

1. What does "Peace starts with me" mean?

2. Explain the rules for brainstorming in your own words.

3. Why is brainstorming important?

4. What are some human differences? Please list some.

5. What are the different ways people keep informed?

6. Why is it important to keep informed?

7. List two well-known peacemakers and describe why they qualify as peacemakers.

8. What have you done in the past month to aid your school, community, or country?

9. Define:

    unique

    dignity

    interconnected

    respect

10. Describe, in your own words, your vision of a "Civilization of Love."

Stage III: Exploring Our Roots And Interconnectedness

"If civilization is to survive, we must culminate the science of human relationships — the ability of all peoples, of all kinds, to live together, in the same world at peace."

Franklin Delano Roosevelt

GROUP BRAINSTORMING — GLOBAL ISSUES

NOTE: Be sure to send home the Letter to Parents (found at the end of this lesson) before proceeding.

OBJECTIVES

- The students will summarize articles they have brought in about other countries, from newspapers or magazines.

- The students will determine the main issue or problem addressed in a selected article.

- The students will brainstorm solutions to the problem in a selected article.

- The students will work collaboratively to reach a conclusion.

- The students will decide upon a plan of action.

MATERIALS

- Student articles
- Map
- One piece of chart paper and marker for each group of five children
- Chalkboard, chalk

PROCEDURE

1. Ask students to sit in a circle and bring their articles. Say, "All year long, we have been looking at how we can take part in having a more peaceful world. Today we're going to look at some global issues. "Go over the words "global" and "issues." Say, "We're going to come up with a solution for at least one of the problems we read about."

2. Ask, "Why is it important for us to know about global issues?" Discuss. Stress that all people are citizens — not only of their communities, their states, and their countries, but also of the world. State, "We are all part of the human family." Ask: "What does being a part of the human family mean to you?"

3. Review the meaning of "interconnectedness." Ask: "How are we interconnected with the environment?" Discuss. Stress our dependency on air, light, food, and water. Ask, "How are we interconnected with one another?" Discuss.

4. Say, "Today we're going to take a careful look at issues and problems of a global nature. We will listen to each other summarize our articles, and then we will focus on one article to brainstorm about."

5. Have each child briefly summarize his/her article, indicating the names of the countries involved and what issue is being addressed.

6. Choose one article on which to focus. Briefly review it and write the problem on the board. Have a child locate the country in the article on the map, naming the countries around it. Name the continent it is on. Have the class break up into problem-solving groups.

7. Have each group choose a leader. The leader will record all brainstorming ideas on a piece of chart paper and share them later.

8. Say, "I'm going to give you five to ten minutes to brainstorm solutions to the problem in the article. Keep in mind the basic needs of

the people in the article. Put yourself in their place and think of what kind of solution you would most want." Distribute chart paper and markers.

9. Give the class brainstorming time. When they have reached a conclusion, have the groups return to the circle, and allow time for each group leader to share solutions. Write the solutions on the board and put a check by the ones that are repeated.

10. Review the entire list of brainstorming solutions. Have the class choose the best ones. Circle them.

11. Ask the class for combinations (if appropriate) of the best solutions to be used toward the final solution.

12. Have the class decide on a final solution. Say, "With whom can we share this so that it can make the most impact?" List every suggestion.

13. Have the class create a plan of action which may involve writing to the president of the country in the article, writing to the UN, writing to the newspapers, etc.

14. Follow through with a plan of action.

15. Follow-up: Display any articles or letters you receive back and send copies to your principal, superintendent, and the parents of your children.

LETTER TO PARENTS
Learning the Skills of Peacemaking
Lesson 40

Dear Parents,

As part of Learning the Skills of Peacemaking, we will be doing a current events lesson on a global problem. Could you assist your child in finding a current events article focusing on a global issue that your child can understand? Please avoid any article that's controversial or that depicts excessive violence. Could you go over the article with your child (read it to him/her if necessary), and make sure your child knows the names of the countries involved and the nature of the problem? In class the children will be "brainstorming" solutions to global problems.

Thanks, as always, for your help.

Sincerely,

_____
Teacher

_____
Date

"I Messages /You Messages" In Global Issues

OBJECTIVES

- The students will act out being people from the country they discussed in Lesson 40.

- The students will use "I/You Messages" in communicating with one another.

- The students will determine which mode of communication works better in dealing with global issues.

MATERIALS

- Win/Win Guidelines poster from Lesson 8
- Journals
- The article discussed in Lesson 40.

PROCEDURE

1. Have the children form a circle. Refer to the article. Say, "What was the problem we discussed in our last lesson? Who were the leaders or people involved?" Discuss.

2. Say, "Today we're going to act out being those people and we're going to use the Win/Win Guidelines to try to work out the problem. We will pretend that we are the actual people involved."

3. Choose several children to come to the center of the circle.

4. Say, "There's one change I'm going to make in the Win/Win Guidelines before we begin. Instead of using 'I Messages,' I want you to use 'You Messages.' Who remembers the difference between 'I' and 'You' Messages?" Discuss. "Who can give an example of each?" Have several examples given.

5. Review the Win/Win Guidelines and proceed

with the enactment of the global conflict.

6. After the enactment, talk about the interaction. Ask the class and the players how using "You Messages" affected the outcome. Discuss.

7. Do the enactment over again using the same children or different ones. This time have them use "I Messages."

8. Talk about how the use of "I Messages" changed the outcome of the conflict. Have the class compare the effectiveness of this enactment with the first one.

9. Encourage the class to draw conclusions as to which mode of communication, "I" or "You" Messages, would work better in global level communication.

10. Have the class write in their journals about the process they just did, and the understandings that came out of it.

WE ARE ALL FROM DIFFERENT PLACES

OBJECTIVES

- Each child will begin to determine his own ethnic background.

- The children will work with relatives or parents in finding out about their "roots."

- The children will begin research projects on at least one country from which their ancestors originated.

- The children will begin to understand that their families represent many different backgrounds.

   NOTE: This lesson, along with Lessons 43 and 44, correlates with Bulletin Board 10 entitled, "Roots Feed the Tree of Life." Hang the tree and the words prior to beginning this lesson.

MATERIALS

- Note to Parents (see Page 150)
- Research project contract (see Page 149)
- Map or globe

PROCEDURE

1. Hand out notes to parents and the research project contracts.

2. Go over the contracts and notes, filling in blanks together. Clearly post the project due date in the room.

3. Refer to the 'Tree of Life' bulletin board. Say, "America is unique in that all of its people originally came from or 'originated' in other places." Explain the word "originated." Tell the children that during the next lesson they will each get a notecard where they will write the name of the country/countries from which they originate. Let them know that their parents will help them with this tonight. Tell them the notecards will be hung on the "Tree of Life" bulletin board during the next lesson.

4. Explain that most people in the United States are the combination of many different backgrounds. Tell the students about your own ethnic background and the countries from which your ancestors originated. Locate these

countries on the map.

5. Ask the students if any of them know about their ethnic origins. Go over the meaning of the word "ethnic." Have those children who know their ethnic background locate the countries from which they originated on the map or globe. Stress, "We are all a part of the human family. We are all interconnected, even to people we don't know. We may have cousins and relatives who still live in other countries. Maybe someday we will meet them. Maybe some of you already have." Discuss.

6. Remind the children that they will find out about their roots from their parents or other relatives. Tell them they need to return the Parent Note with the information about their background in two days. Tell them that when they present their reports to the class they can bring in anything they have to illustrate their backgrounds: pictures, books, articles of clothing, coins, dolls, pictures of relatives who immigrated here. Tell them that as an optional

activity they can bring in a native food (enough for the class to taste) on the day of their presentation.

7. Tell the children they will be locating more "countries of origin" on the map in the next lesson. Make sure the children fully understand the term "countries of origin."

> NOTE: Children of mixed ethnic backgrounds should choose one country to research. Any child unsure of his/her background can either research the appropriate continent or state.

RESEARCH PROJECT CONTRACT
Learning the Skills of Peacemaking
Lesson 42

I _____, agree to complete my research

project on:_____ by_____.
                                                    date
I agree to get the help I need to complete this assignment. I also agree to speak to my teacher if I have any problems.

Signature _____

Date _____

NOTE TO PARENTS
Learning the Skills of Peacemaking
Lesson 42

Dear Parents,

   As part of Learning the Skills of Peacemaking, your child will be completing and written project on one country from which his/her ancestors originated. Please help your child list the name(s) of the countries in his/her ethnic background on the attached form and return it by _____. If your child's background includes several different countries, only one will be chosen to work on. If you are uncertain of your ancestral roots, your child can do research on our state or the continent your ancestor came from. In order to complete the project, your child will need the following information:

- A map of his/her country of origin to copy from a book, encyclopedia, or from an actual map
- On what continent is the country?
- What does the flag look like? Have your child draw it.
- What kind of native dress does the country have? Describe it. Draw or make an example.
- What are the native foods?

   As an optional activity you can help your child prepare an ethnic dish to bring to school on the day of his/her report presentation.

- What other interesting facts can your child tell us about his or her country of origin?
- Could you please help your child gather the necessary information. The report should be written in his/her own words. Suggested length is _____ pages.

                                                Thank you,

                                                _____
                                                Teacher

COUNTRIES OF ORIGIN
Learning the Skills of Peacemaking
Lesson 42

Child's Name _____

Country(ies) of Origin_____

_____

_____

_____

_____

_____

_____

_____

_____

I will help my child locate information about his/her country of origin. I understand

that his/her completed project is due on: _____

I will send in an ethnic dish:

Yes_____   No_____

_____

Parent's Signature

Please return this note to school.

Bulletin Board 10
Learning the Skills of Peacemaking

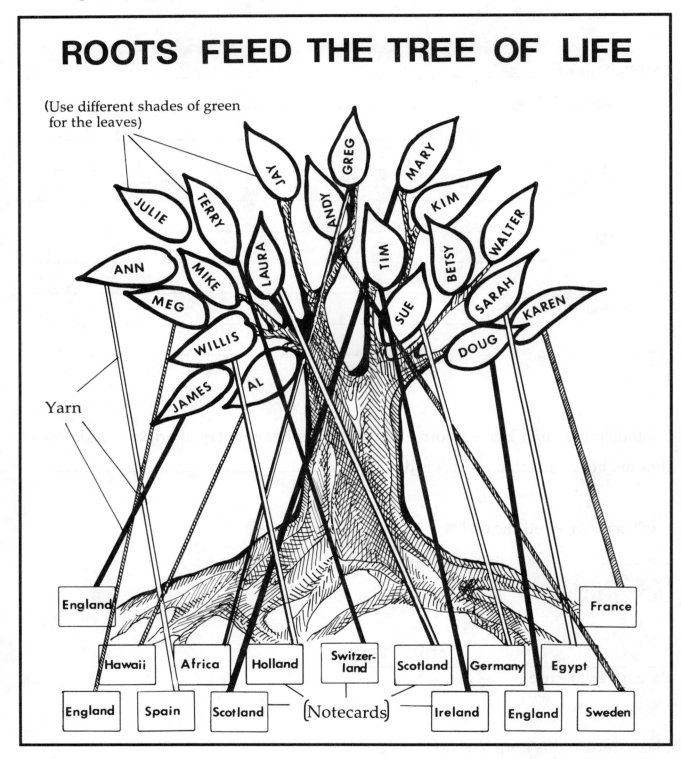

COUNTRIES OF ORIGIN

OBJECTIVES

• The children will locate countries of origin on a map or globe.

• The children will understand that there are people with many different backgrounds in their own classroom (neighborhood, country, world).

MATERIALS

• "Countries of Origin" papers from Lesson 42

• A note card for each child

• World map or large globe

• Yarn, clay, labels

• Large paper entitled: "We Are From Many Different Places"

• "Tree of Life" bulletin board

PROCEDURE

1. Have the children sit in a circle. Say, "We all have relatives or ancestors who came to the United States from other lands." Remind them that these lands are called 'countries of origin.' Say, "You brought notes home a few days ago asking your parents to help you determine your countries of origin." Go around the circle and have the children name their countries of origin. Have each go to the map and locate one of his/her countries of origin. Hand each child a note card after he/she does this, and instruct him/her to write the name of that country on the top left. This will be the country he/she will research. Underline it. Beneath it have the child write his/her other countries of origin. Have the children write their names on the top right. In Lesson 44, these note cards will be hung on the "Tree of Life" bulletin board. Refer to the bulletin board and show the children where their cards will be displayed.

2. Have each child attach a piece of yarn (with clay on each end) to the United States and the country of origin he/she will be researching. By the end of the lesson, there should be a piece of yarn for every child's selected country of origin.

3. Complete the poster "We Are All from Many Different Places" by listing the children's names and all of his/her countries of origin. Explain that even though each child will only be

researching one country, all of his/her countries of origin will be recorded on the chart.

4. Say, "We are all part of one earth. We are the human family. Our ancestors came to the United States from other countries. We now live in harmony in America, just as people of the whole earth may someday live in harmony." Ask, "What does living in harmony mean to you?"

LIVING IN HARMONY

OBJECTIVES

- The children will explore the concept of living in harmony.
- The children will explore the concept of the UN as an instrument of harmony.
- The children will further explore their roots and interconnectedness.

MATERIALS

- "We Are All from Different Places" chart
- Encyclopedia — "United Nations" section
- "Tree of Life" bulletin board including a leaf with the name of each child, and yarn
- Notecards the children have filled out with name of country they are researching and their other countries of origin
- Globe with clay and yarn attached
- Chalkboard, chalk

PROCEDURE

1. Have the children sit in a circle. Go over the "We Are from Many Different Places" chart, stressing the broad background of the class and how many countries they represent.

2. Review the concept of "living in harmony" that was discussed in Lesson 44. Ask the children what "living in harmony" means to them.

3. Draw the analogy to musical harmony, in which different instruments work together to make one unified sound, yet each participating instrument is inherently different. Make sure the children understand this analogy.

4. Briefly discuss the United Nations as "an instrument of harmony." Using the encyclopedia, show children pictures of the UN. Describe its function. Discuss.

5. Say, "We work together in harmony in our class. Many of us are from different backgrounds, but in many ways we are alike." Ask, "How are we alike?" Discuss. List common qualities on the board.

6. Refer to the note cards mentioned in Lessons 42 and 43 on which the children have written their countries of origin. Have each child come to the "Tree of Life" bulletin board and hang up their note cards.

7. Continue to talk about the class members' diverse background. Draw parallels among members of the class, noting children's similar roots. Also note the diversity and how rich the class is in different cultures. Remind the children of the due dates of their completed projects. Tell them that they will be presenting their reports orally to the class. Remind them to bring in any objects, pictures or artifacts that relate to their countries. Remind them also to bring in their ethnic foods at this time if they have chosen to do this optional part of the report.

   NOTE: Have a special area set aside in the room for the children to display their projects and matching artifacts, etc. Indicate to the children that everything they bring in will be displayed.

8. Have the students look at the "Tree of Life" bulletin board, now complete. Say, "Notice all of the different countries we come from. The "Tree of Life" is like our country and our earth. We are all interconnected."

ORAL REPORTS: OUR COUNTRIES OF ORIGIN

OBJECTIVES

- The children will deliver their oral reports on their country of origin

- The children will gain a deeper understanding of the diversity of their backgrounds.

    NOTE: This lesson can take several days, allowing a group of children each day to present their reports. This is recommended if the reports tend to be lengthy so the class doesn't get bored.

MATERIALS

- Children's reports and related visuals
- Map/globe
- Optional — paper plates, napkins, plastic forks, or spoons

PROCEDURE

1. The children can either remain in their seats or form a circle for the delivery of the oral reports. Tell them that every child will get a turn to present their report, and that the rest of the class is invited to ask questions or provide added information during each presentation.

2. Have each child deliver his/her report. Have him/her locate the country he/she researched on the map or globe during the presentation.

3. If the children have brought in ethnic foods, have them serve the food after the report has been presented.

THE LADDER OF PEACEMAKING

OBJECTIVES

- The children will understand the hierarchy of peacemaking.

- The children will understand the connection between individual and global acts.

- The children will be guided to take responsibility for the world beyond themselves.

  NOTE: This lesson correlates with Bulletin Board 11 entitled: "The Ladder of Peacemaking."

MATERIALS

- Chart

"Things You Can Do To Express Peacemaking":

Treat others as you want to be treated.

Accept others.

Work together cooperatively.

Solve your conflicts non-violently.

Be aware that we are all part of the same human family.

- Copy of The Bill of Rights from the encyclopedia

- Eight pieces of paper in graduated sizes with the following written on each from smallest to largest:

  The Individual

  You & Me

  Us (small groups)

  Our Community

  Our Country

  Our State

  Our Continent

  Our World

- Masking tape to be used to attach the nine papers

PROCEDURE

1. Have the students sit in a circle. Direct the students' attention to "The Ladder of Peacemaking" bulletin board.

2. Say, "The ladder represents peace in the world and how we play a part in getting there. Picture yourself as the person holding up this ladder." Ask, "What would happen if you let go of the ladder?" (It would fall down.) Say, "So it is with peacemaking. Individuals need to take responsibility for having a peaceful world. The individual is the foundation of a peaceful world. At the base of the ladder you can enable peace

to happen at many different levels:

- within yourself
- with others
- in your communities
- in your state, country, and in the world

3. Point to the next level of the ladder, "You and Me." Show the chart: "Things You Can Do To Express Peacemaking." Discuss these concepts.

4. Say, "Let's look at the next step on the ladder, 'Us'." This step stands for the fact that you as an individual can make a difference in small groups. Ask, "What are some of the small groups you are involved in?" Refer back to the chart, "Things You Can Do To Express Peacemaking." Have the children relate the concepts on the chart to the way they interact in small groups. Talk about cooperation and acceptance at this level.

5. Focus on the next step of the ladder, "county, community, state, and country." Guide your students to see that they have a contribution to make at each of these levels, and they have already done this through some of the activities in other lessons. Discuss. Ask, "How can you take responsibility and get involved in the workings of your community, state, and country?" This is a good place to stress letter writing, knowledge of current events, attending town meetings, voting.

6. Ask about "the right to vote." Ask what this means. Discuss the privilege the citizens of this country have to cast their vote, and to have a say in the course of human events.

7. Refer to this country's Bill of Rights. Show a picture of it from an encyclopedia. Briefly explain what it means. Paraphrase each "right" to your class. Discuss. Say, "Being a peacemaker means exercising one's rights. Through this we are both taking responsibility for and making a contribution to the world around us."

8. Move up to the top of the ladder — "Our Continent and Our World." Define the term "global citizen" as someone who is part of the whole human family. Say, "Being a global citizen means that we are all citizens of the planet earth. We are interconnected, we share the earth together. Through our ability to communicate with one another we can actually be in touch with people across the globe." Ask, "What are some of the forms of communication we have that connect us globally?" (Some responses might be: TV, radio, computers, satellite communications, the mail, air travel, the telephone.)

9. Say, "It's possible to share information and even to solve problems together through joint efforts. What are some of the global problems we could work on together?" (Some responses might be: hunger, war, poverty, homelessness, diseases, pollution, crime, illiteracy.) Ask, "How can you make a difference in any of these areas?" Discuss.

> NOTE: This is a great time to pick a class project which will enable the children to address global problem solving. Choose the problem of greatest concern to the class. Brainstorm "action steps." Decide when to begin the project.

10. Pass the nine pieces of graduated sized paper to different children. This is done to reinforce the concepts you just went over on the bulletin board. Have each child read the caption on the paper. Ask the children to arrange the papers on the floor in the order indicated through the "Ladder of Peacemaking" discussion.

11. When the papers are arranged in the correct order, hand strips of tape to other students and have them transfer the papers to the wall. Hang the papers up in order. A "free time" activity can be having two children at a time point to each paper, discussing how they personally can express peacemaking at each level.

12. In concluding the lesson, guide the class to reiterate that each segment of the hierarchy or "Ladder of Peacemaking" depends on the one preceding it, and the individual is at the foundation.

Bulletin Board 11
Learning the Skills of Peacemaking

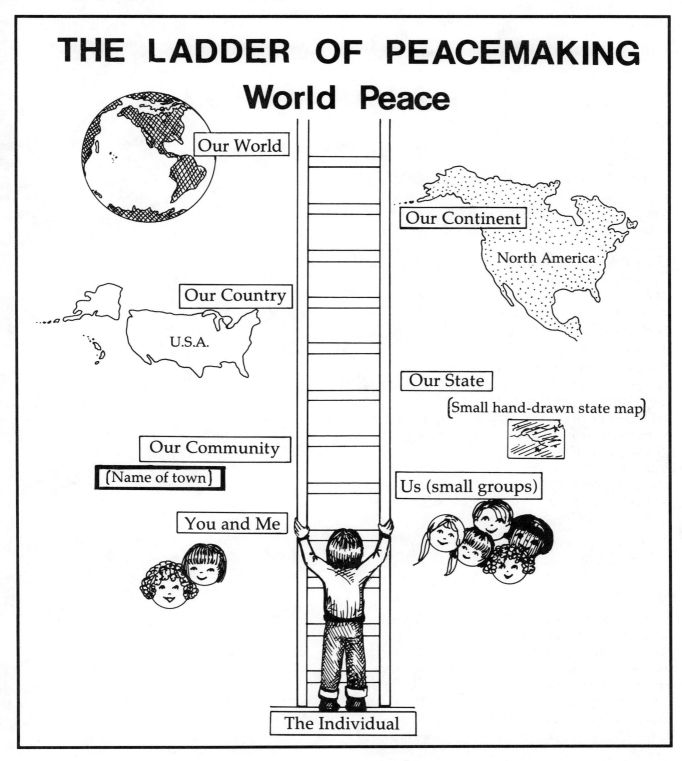

THE LADDER OF PEACEMAKING
World Peace

Our World

Our Continent

North America

Our Country

U.S.A.

Our State

(Small hand-drawn state map)

Our Community

(Name of town)

Us (small groups)

You and Me

The Individual

WE ARE DIFFERENT, WE ARE THE SAME

OBJECTIVES

- The children will identify differences and similarities in each other's thinking during a conflict resolution exercise.

- The children will use the technique of role reversal in problem solving.

MATERIALS

- Clipboard, paper, pens

PROCEDURE

NOTE: Do steps 1 and 2 first thing in the morning. The rest of the lesson is done at the end of the day.

1. Say, "As global citizens we must always be aware of our individual responsibility in solving conflicts that come up between us. Today we're going to learn a new way of doing this."

2. Say, "When you have difficulty solving a problem with another member of the class you may sign up on this clipboard (hold up). Please write the date, your name, the name of the other student involved, and a brief statement of your problem without placing blame."

3. At the end of the day have the class gather in a circle. Bring the clipboard into the circle.

4. Say, "How many of you have had a conflict today and signed up on the clipboard? What did you do to solve your conflict?" Give time for discussion. Talk about what worked, what didn't work. Say, "We're going to use a new technique for problem solving and conflict resolution. This time you can pretend to be the other person so that you can see the problem from someone else's point of view." Refer to the clipboard.

5. Say, "Today _____ and _____ had a conflict. Please come to the center of the circle. Now _____ pretend to be _____ and _____ pretend to be_____ . You are going to switch roles and act out the conflict."

6. Guide them in acting out what they perceived the other person to be doing and feeling.

7. When this is complete let both students sit back down in the circle. Have the class discuss what happened. Talk about how people may have different points of view but we all want to be loved and respected by others.

8. Guide the children to recognize that although people may have differences, they can resolve problems by seeing the other's point of view. Let the children who switched roles tell what they realized when they pretended to be the other person.

9. Try this technique as often as you wish. You can have the clipboard and role reversal time as an ongoing part of your class activity. Some teachers do this several times a week.

BEING GLOBAL CITIZENS

OBJECTIVES

- The students will represent different foreign countries in groups.

- The students will work collaboratively to determine what are the most important needs on a global scale for the country they represent.

- The students will act as foreign ministers of the countries they represent.

- The students will reach an agreement, as a class, on priority global needs and their solutions.

  NOTE: Each child needs a current events article prior to this lesson. You may wish to draft a note to parents ahead of time asking them to assist their child in locating an article dealing with a foreign country, determining the problem, and perceiving the needs of the country.

MATERIALS

- Student's current events articles dealing with a foreign country

- Large chart paper and markers for each group of five

- Journals

- Paper and pencils for "Foreign Ministers"

- Chalkboard, chalk

PROCEDURE

1. Have students bring their current events articles to the circle.

2. Ask each child to briefly tell about the article, including the country it focuses on, the problem outlined, and any perceived needs that country might have.

3. Choose four or five different countries featured in the articles. Go over the problem described in each article. Write the name of each country on the board. Beneath it, write the problem referred to in the article. Divide the class into teams representing each of the countries listed on the board. Give each team chart paper and a marker and a paper and pencil for the foreign minister. Have the team pick both a leader who will record information and a "Minister of Foreign Affairs."

4. Create the scenario: "You are getting ready for a special meeting at the United Nations during which you will be speaking to representatives of other countries about the most pressing world problems and how to solve them. You will be given an unlimited amount of money to solve whatever problems you see as the most crucial for the world in general. In your group, choose the top three world problems and a proposed solution for each of them. Try to remember what the special problems of your country might be. After eight minutes we will stop." Distribute the chart paper and markers. Have the children write the name of the country they are representing on the top of the chart. Beneath it have them write what they perceive to be the three most pressing global problems. They should be thinking in terms of the country they are representing as well as general global problems. The children should be encouraged to draw upon their knowledge of urgent world problems such as hunger, disease, violence, etc.

5. Allow time for the groups to discuss, brainstorm, and record the problems. Then ask them to list the top three problems and a possible solution for each. Circulate and help mediate differences as they arise. Foreign minister lists everything on his/her paper.

6. After eight minutes say, "Now we're going to listen to the list of problems and solutions each country has come up with." Have each group leader share the problems and solutions.

7. Say, "Now each Foreign Minister will visit one other country (group) and discuss the lists drawn up, seeing if the country you visit agrees or disagrees with your list. At the end of this activity we will make an imaginary visit to the UN with the lists and decide as a group on the top three world problems and proposed solutions."

8. Give the Foreign Minister five minutes to visit other "countries." Countries can make changes in their lists at this time.

9. Now, have the class role play being at the UN. They can sit in groups representing their country. Let foreign ministers present revised lists and explain the process they went through in revision.

10. Ask the class (UN delegates) to vote on the top three global problems and solutions for them. Have them discuss the process used to get to this point of agreement or disagreement.

11. Ask, "What must it be like for real UN delegates in working to solve global problems?"

12. Students write in their journals and describe how they felt during this process. Was it difficult to come to agreement with others in and out of their own group? What worked? What didn't work? Do they think it's possible for real countries to work out their differences?

FINDING SOLUTIONS TO WORLD CONFLICT, PART 1

OBJECTIVES

- The children will begin preparation for an exercise in global conflict resolution.

- The children will be divided into five groups to represent different sides of global issues. The groups will represent Israel, a selected Arab country, U.S., and the U.S.S.R. There will also be a mediation panel of two students.

MATERIALS

- Two recent articles in the news, one on U.S./Soviet conflict, the other on conflict between Israel and a selected Arab country

- Four large pieces of paper, one for each area represented, for maps to be drawn on

- A map of the United States, Soviet Union, Israel, and the same Arab country focused on in your current events article. The children will copy these maps.

- Markers, crayons, and paints

- Letter to parents (see Page 169)

PROCEDURE

1. Have the students form a circle. Say, "We've spent some time discussing global problems and solutions to them. Today we're going to prepare to look at the issue of global conflict, particularly with the United States, the Soviet Union, Israel, and (selected Arab county).

2. Ask the children what they know about issues of conflict between the United States and the Soviet Union. Encourage the children to discuss what they see as the basic issues of conflict. Be aware of stereotypes and misrepresentations.

3. Ask the children about Israel and the Middle East. See what they know about the issues of conflict there. Again, be aware of stereotypes.

4. Hold up the articles you brought in about the U.S./Soviet conflict and an Israeli/Arabic conflict. Tell the children that in the next lesson they will be divided into groups to represent these areas of the world. Tell them that you will be reviewing the articles with them in order to give them some background on these areas of conflict.

5. Go over the article on U.S./Soviet conflict. Briefly discuss it together.

6. Next, go over the article on an Israeli/Arabic conflict. Discuss it briefly.

7. Tell the children that you will be dividing them into groups to represent the U.S., U.S.S.R., Israel, and the Arab country selected. Let them know, as well, that two children will serve as mediators and they will help the opposing groups use mediation guidelines to work out conflicts during the next lesson.

8. Divide the class into four groups of equal size, with two children left over to serve as mediators.

9. Give each group their large piece of paper on which to draw the map of the country they represent. Distribute markers, crayons and paints. Give each group a real map to copy from.

10. Tell the children that creating their map is a peacemaking activity, and have them describe the way they plan to work together as peacemakers. Stress cooperation, consideration, and care.

11. Have the children create their maps while you meet with the mediators.

12. Tell the mediators that they will be helping the opposing sides come to an agreement. They will also be choosing people to take turns speaking from each side, much as a judge would do in a court of law. The procedure that the mediators will follow is to have each side:

> a. State the problem as they see it.
>
> b. State how the other side sees it.
>
> c. Brainstorm solutions (have someone record).
>
> d. Have both sides decide on a solution that's mutually satisfying.

Coach the mediators on how to utilize the above mediation guidelines with the groups. Do some role play together. Make sure the mediators are comfortable with their jobs. Decide whether or not they'll need another coaching session before the actual lesson. If so, arrange one. Select one mediator for U.S./U.S.S.R. and one for Israel/Arab county.

13. After the groups have finished their maps, have them re-assemble in a circle. Tell them that each child is to locate an article about the country they represent; e.g., the children representing the Soviet Union will find an article about the Soviet Union. Remind the children that the article should deal with a conflict that country is having with its opponent.

14. Tell the children that after they've read their articles they will be bringing them in to school and trading them with other members of their group, so that each child will have the opportunity to go over at least one other article. In the meantime you, as teacher, can be collecting articles on all the countries involved for the children to look at in class.

NOTE: When the articles are brought in, copy two from each country that the mediators will be handling. The mediator who will be handling the U.S./U.S.S.R. will get two articles each about the U.S. and U.S.S.R. The other mediator will get two articles each about Israel and the selected Arab country.

15. Before the next lesson, give all groups a chance to get together and trade articles to bring home. They can also talk about what they have already read. This will be a good time to meet with the mediators and go over the mediation guidelines one more time. Also, answer any questions the mediators might have about the country they will be working with.

16. Distribute copies of the Letter to Parents (see Page 169). Encourage the children to have their parents go over the articles with them ahead of time.

LETTER TO PARENTS
Learning the Skill of Peacemaking
Lesson 49

Dear Parents,

    We are going to be representing different countries during a lesson on world conflict. Would you help me find, read and understand a current events article on _____ (country).

    Soon I will be trading articles with other children. I will need your help then as well. Thanks for helping me learn more about the world in which we live.

                        Love,

                        Student's Name

FINDING SOLUTIONS TO WORLD CONFLICT, PART II

OBJECTIVES

- Students will engage in a simulation in which they represent Israel, a selected Arab country, U.S., and the U.S.S.R.

- The students will determine the top conflict between the country they represent and its opponent. They will propose solutions to the problem.

- The mediators will work with opposing countries to come up with a joint solution, using the mediation guidelines.

MATERIALS

- One large handmade map of each place: U.S., U.S.S.R., Israel, and the selected Arab country (from Lesson 49)

- Current event articles the children have brought in

- Chart paper and markers for each group

- Clipboard and pencil for each mediator

- Journals

- Copy of mediation guidelines for each mediator. See Lesson 49.

- Teacher's notepad and pen

PROCEDURE

1. Ask each country to sit in an opposite corner of the room around its map. Ask each mediator to sit with one of the countries they will be working with. Mediators then go the other country five minutes later. They just listen at this time.

2. Have each country select a leader who will write down on chart paper the top problem the country faces regarding its adversary (U.S./U.S.S.R./ Israel/Arab country) based on the reading done in the articles and discussions in class. Distribute chart paper and markers and allow ten minutes for each group to come up with possible solutions for this problem. Allow about ten minutes for this process.

3. After the students have recorded the problem and solutions on their charts, have each group take its map and meet with its opposing group in a "neutral" place.

4. Ask the mediators to go to the groups and begin the process of mediation. The objective is that the opposing groups will come up with a solution for the conflicts they have with each other. Allow fifteen minutes for mediation time. The mediators will have each side do the following:

a. State the problem as they see it

b. State the problem as the other side sees it.

c. Brainstorm solutions (choose one child to record).

d. Decide on a solution that suits both parties.

  NOTE: Opposing sides may see the top problem differently. They might have to come up with a variety of solutions.

5. Circulate among the groups and, if possible, have an "outside advisor" present to sit with the groups as well (a parent, teacher's aide, the principal, or special subject teacher). Take notes on the process. Write down what happens when the groups are deadlocked. (The notes will be used in the next lesson.) Write down what happens when one group tries to influence the other. Do they force, cajole, conciliate, threaten, withdraw? Also write down how effective the mediator's efforts are. Can the mediator move the group toward agreement? Why or why not?

6. After fifteen minutes, the mediator announces either the solutions or the failure to

reach an agreement. You can have a brief discussion at this time, but the major follow-up will take place during the next lesson.

7. Have the children return to their seats and write in their journals. Have them describe their thoughts, feelings, and actions during the process.

FINDING SOLUTIONS TO WORLD CONFLICT, PART III

OBJECTIVES

- The students will describe their thoughts, feelings, and reactions during Lesson 50.

- The children will gain an understanding of problems encountered by countries involved in global conflict situations.

MATERIALS

- Teachers notes from Lesson 50
- Journals

PROCEDURE

1. Ask the children to sit in a circle and relate their experiences in the mediation session from Lesson 50. Ask how it felt to be the different countries they each represented. Discuss.

2. Ask the mediators what it was like to try to mediate the conflicts. Discuss. Encourage each child to examine his/her thoughts, feelings, and reactions.

3. If the process worked and an agreement was reached, ask the children how they reached their agreement. Discuss the process. Refer to your own notes taken during the mediation process in Lesson 50 and share your observations with the class. Your "outside advisors" can be present to contribute their reactions as well.

4. If an agreement was not reached, discuss this, and ask the children to pinpoint the breakdowns and deadlocks in the process. Ask what might have worked.

5. Ask the class, "Do you feel that nations can actively work out disputes by talking things out?" Discuss.

6. Have students examine the above question in their journals, commenting on the process and making suggestions.

INTRODUCING ROLE REVERSAL IN GLOBAL CONFLICT

OBJECTIVES

- The children will prepare to assume the role of the "opposing" country they worked with in Lesson 51.

- The children will trade articles relating to the country they now represent.

- The mediators will prepare to work with the countries they didn't work with during Lesson 51.

- The children will make maps of the countries they now represent.

MATERIALS

- The current events articles the children have already read on the U.S., U.S.S.R., Israel, and a selected Arab country

- A large paper for each group to make a map of the country they represent

- Markers, paints, crayons

- Real maps to copy from representing the U.S., U.S.S.R., Israel and the selected Arab country.

PROCEDURE

1. Have the children bring their current events articles and sit in a circle. Tell them that during the next lesson they will be taking on the role of the country they opposed during the last lesson. Discuss, and allow the children's reactions to surface.

2. Tell the class that this activity is designed to enable them to understand what it's like to be "in the shoes" of the other country. Discuss this concept.

3. Have the children get into the groups they represented in the last lesson. Say, "United States you are now the Soviet Union. Soviet Union, you are now the United States. Israel, you are now _____ . (Arab country you have chosen). _____ you are now Israel.

4. Say, "In order to understand more about the country you will now be representing, I'm going to ask you to trade articles with the children who represented that country during Lesson 51." Have the children who represented the U.S./U.S.S.R. trade articles with each other. Children representing Israel/Arab country trade as well. Mediators also trade copies of the articles they have read.

5. Tell the class, "Tonight I'd like you to read the article you just traded, and ask your parents to help you with anything you don't

understand. As you are reading, try to remember that you now represent this country." Discuss briefly.

6. Pass out the map papers, drawing/painting materials, and the real map to copy from.

7. Have the children work on their maps together while you meet with the mediators to discuss plans for the next session.

ROLE REVERSALS IN GLOBAL CONFLICT

OBJECTIVES

- The students will reverse roles and will be involved in the mediation of a global conflict involving U.S./U.S.S.R., Israel/Arab country.

- The students will experience what it is like to be "in the shoes" of the country who was their adversary in the last process.

MATERIALS

- Large map the children have made of the country they represent

- Mediation guidelines

- Clipboard and pen for each mediator

- Notepad and pen for the teacher

PROCEDURE

1. Ask the students to take positions around the map of their country in opposite corners of the room.

2. Have each country choose a leader who will record the top problem of that country in the area of conflict with the opposing side. They also record solutions to that problem. This should take about ten minutes.

3. The mediators will sit and listen to each group they will be with, spending about five minutes with each. You rotate and take notes on the process. If you can arrange to have outside advisors present (a parent, another teacher, the principal, etc.), they can be seated with the different groups, taking notes as well. Remember, you will use your notes in the follow-up discussion.

4. After ten minutes, have the opposing sides meet in a "neutral" area. Have each mediator go to that area. The mediators will have each side:

   a. State the problem as they see it.

   b. State how the other side feels about the problem.

   c. Brainstorm solutions.

   d. Have both sides decide on a solution that satisfies all parties involved.

5. After fifteen minutes, the mediators announce that an agreement was reached, or failure to reach an agreement.

6. Have the students form a circle to discuss the process. Use your own notes at this time. Have the mediators describe their experiences. Ask the children what they felt worked and didn't work in trying to come up with joint solutions. Discuss.

7. Ask the children what they learned about themselves in this process. Discuss.

8. Ask the children how their experience in this lesson was different from the last, when they represented the opposing side.

9. Have the children describe their feelings and reactions in their journals.

MURALS: ENVISIONING A WORLD AT PEACE

OBJECTIVES

- The students will use the process of "imaging" to create their vision of a world at peace.

- The students will combine their individual visions into two unified class visions in creating the murals.

MATERIALS

- Two or three large mural papers — one piece for each group of twelve students

- Pastel chalk, markers, crayons, paint

PROCEDURE

1. Have the children sit in a large circle. Say, "Today we are going to imagine what the world would look like if it were perfectly peaceful." Say, "Close your eyes and picture your neighborhood this way — peaceful in all aspects with the environment being cared for, also. Picture our country at peace, with all the people being taken care of."

2. Say, "Now, picture our earth— whole, beautiful, and peaceful. Picture the people of the earth as one big family — the human family. Picture the children of different countries playing together. Picture yourself with them. Let the image take shape and grow. I'm going to give you a few minutes to picture in your mind your vision of a world at peace." Give the children about three minutes of silence.

3. Wait a few moments. Say, "Now open your eyes. What did you see?" Discuss.

4. After the children have had sufficient time to share their visions, say, "Now we will form two large groups to work together in creating a mural of your visions of a world at peace." Ask the children to select group leaders. Say, "The creation of these murals will reflect your ability to work together as peacemakers. You will want to combine all your separate visions into one unified whole in each mural. Work with your group leader to determine together what the basic elements of your mural will be (sun, horizon line, mountains, water. Please don't "put down" anyone's ideas. See how well you can combine many different ideas, and have them all fit together."

5. Distribute mural paper and materials. Say, "Each of you will get to express your own visions of peace in these murals. But all separate visions should flow into one unified theme. If someone's idea is different than your own, allow it to be and consider the possibilities this idea has for working with your own."

6. Stress that the creation of these murals is a peacemaking activity. It involves different people working together, sharing ideas, and solving problems as they arise. Say, "Perhaps, peace will come to the world when all people can work together cooperatively."

7. Have the groups discuss ways they will execute their murals. You can "coach," but all the creating and the problem solving should come from the children.

8. Allow the children to take as long as they need. Set aside an afternoon for this project if needed, or have the class work on the murals for several consecutive days. Clean up should also be a collaborative activity.

9. Follow up when the murals are completed: call in the local newspapers to take pictures and then display the murals in the school library.

DESIGNING A WORLD FLAG

OBJECTIVES

- The children will work cooperatively in groups to create and design world flags.

- The children will describe what they feel is needed to have a world at peace.

MATERIALS

- Chart entitled: "This is What's Needed to Have a World at Peace." (Children's ideas will go here.)

- Four or five large white papers - (suggested size: 3' X 4') for flags

- Crayons, markers, rulers, paints

- Camera, film

PROCEDURE

1. Say, "We have learned about the different countries from which we originated and the different flags of many lands. Today we're going to make world flags. They will be your creation entirely. We're also going to make a chart describing what we feel is needed to have world peace. Pictures of our flags and copies of our chart will be mailed to the Secretary General of the United Nations. In a moment we'll be dividing into groups to do this."

2. Say, "Before we begin I'd like to know why you think we don't have a world flag already." Discuss.

3. Ask the class if they think it's possible to have all of the countries of the world getting along in their lifetimes. Discuss.

4. Say, "What do you think will help us to have a world at peace?" List the ideas on the chart: This is What's Needed to Have a World at Peace. As you are doing the chart together, guide the children to the concept of individual responsibility. Also, guide them to recall the concept of human interconnectedness.

5. After you have completed the chart, say, "Imagine a flag representing all people and all countries. What would it look like?" Have the children close their eyes for a few moments to envision this.

6. Now have the class divide into four groups. Give each group a piece of paper and markers,

etc. to create their flag. Have the children discuss their ideas together. Give them about five to ten minutes to come up with a design concept for their flag.

7. Have the groups design their flag together. Give them about twenty minutes to do this, having the members of the group decide how to execute their ideas.

8. When each group completes their flag, take a picture of it. Have the class write a letter to the Secretary General of the United Nations telling him about the program they've been participating in this year. In the letter, have the children describe how they came up with their idea for the world flag. They can also include suggestions they have for having a world at peace. When you mail copies of the letters and pictures of the flags be sure to include a copy of the chart, "This is What's Needed to Have a World at Peace."

9. The address to send everything to is:

Secretary General
United Nations
New York, New York 10017

Good Luck!

COMMITMENTS FOR THE FUTURE

OBJECTIVES

• The students will make commitments stating how they will personally contribute to having a peaceful world now and in the future.

• The students will record in their journals their role in creating a peaceful future.

MATERIALS

• Chart paper entitled: "What I'd Most Like to Contribute to Our World"

• Journals

PROCEDURE

1. Have the children sit in a circle. Say, "Our school year is ending and we have learned a lot about ourselves and our world." Ask, "What have you learned that you can do to create a peaceful future?" Discuss.

2. Ask, "Do you feel that you can make a difference in the world?" Discuss.

3. Ask, "Do you feel that you can make a contribution regardless of your age? How?" Discuss.

4. Ask, "In your personal lives, how can you create a more peaceful world?" Discuss.

5. Ask, "In your communities, how can you contribute?" Discuss.

6. Ask, "How can you contribute to your country?" Discuss.

7. Ask, "In the world, how can you contribute?" Discuss.

8. Say, "Close your eyes and envision what is the largest contribution you can make to the world in which we live either as a child or as an adult. Think of the thing you most would want to accomplish to make our world a better place. Picture yourself accomplishing this." Allow for a few minutes of silence.

9. Say, "Open your eyes and turn to the person you are sitting next to. Tell your partner what it is that you want to contribute most to the world. Describe how you would like to accomplish this."

10. Give about four to five minutes for paired sharing.

11. Have the children face each other in the circle again. Each child shares about the contribution he or she most wants to make to the world. Record each child's response on the chart: "What I'd Most Like to Contribute to Our World."

12. Ask the children if they would be willing to commit to living this vision of contribution. Say, "When we take a stand to do something important, that's the beginning of making it really happen. When we write down our commitments it is even more powerful."

13. Say, "Today is our opportunity to take a stand for the future."

14. Ask your children to write their commitments to the future in their journals. Give them the opportunity to read their commitments aloud. Acknowledge each child for his/her courage, vision and uniqueness.

15. Say, "Remember you are the key to a peaceful world."

16. Read the following quote by Goethe:

> "Whatever you do, or dream you can do, begin it. Boldness has genius, power and magic in it."

MEASURING THE UNDERSTANDINGS LEARNED IN THIS GUIDE

STAGE III: Exploring Our Roots And Interconnectedness

NOTE: Teachers, you can do this as a recap and review, or you can put these questions on a worksheet to use as a post test.

- Define:

  conflict resolution

  countries of origin

  United Nations

  harmony

  — Tell what the mediation guidelines are in your own words.

  — Do you think mediation can help settle disputes? Why or why not?

  — How are you like other people?

  — Describe the Ladder of Peacemaking.

  — What kind of contribution do you plan to make to the future of our world?

  — If you could speak to our President, what would you tell him?

CONCLUSION

William Ryan, writer and Associate Secretary for Public Affairs, USCC, stated:

"The same values that commit one to be a peacemaker will be the values that impel one to foster the integral development of every human being and of all peoples."

Each time you reach out to your children and students through words and actions, picture your reach far exceeding the walls of the home and classroom. Envision yourself impacting people all over through each interaction you have. And from this vantage point, know that each life you touch will in turn touch others, and this touching of human being to human being may well be the beginning of peace for the whole world.

BIBLIOGRAPHY

Adams, Linda, *Effectiveness Training for Women*. New York: Weyden Books, 1979.

Bickmore, Kathy, *Alternatives to Violence: A Manual for Teaching Peace to Youth and Adults*. Cleveland, Ohio: Alternatives to Violence Committee of the Cleveland Friends Meeting, 1984.

Briggs, Dorothy Corkill, *Your Child's Self-Esteem*. Garden City, New York: Doubleday, 1967.

Canfield, Jack and Wells, Harold, *100 Ways to Enhance Self-Concepts in the Classroom: Handbook for Teachers and Parents*. Englewood Cliffs, New Jersey: Prentice-Hall, Inc., 1976.

Cousins, Norman, *Human Options*. New York: W.W. Norton, 1981.

Dodson, Dr. Fitzhugh, *How to Discipline with Love*. New York: New American Library, Signet, 1978.

Dorn, Lois, *Peace in the Family: A Workbook of Ideas and Actions*. New York: Pantheon, 1983.

Educators for Social Responsibility, *Perspectives*. Boston, Mass.: E.S.R., 1983.

Faber, Adele and Mazlish, Elaine, *How to Talk So Kids Will Listen and Listen So Kids Will Talk*. New York: Rawson, Wade Publishers, 1980.

Fisher, Roger and Ury, William, *Getting to Yes: Negotiating Agreement Without Giving In*. New York: Penguin Book, 1981.

Ginott, Haim, *Teacher and Child*. New York: Avon, 1972.

Gordon, Thomas, *Parent Effectiveness Training*. New York: Peter Weyden, 1970.

Keyes, Ken, Jr., *The Hundreth Monkey*. Kentucky: Vision Books, 1986.

James, Muriel and Jongeward, Dorothy, *Born to Win*. Menlo Park, Calif.: Addison-Wesley, 1971.

Johnson, Spencer, *One Minute for Myself*. New York: William Morrow and Co., 1985.

Knight, Michael E., et al, *Teaching Children to Love Themselves: A Handbook for Parents and Teachers of Young Children*. Englewood Cliffs, N.J.: Prentice-Hall, 1982.

Macy, Joanna Rogers, *Despair and Personal Power in the Nuclear Age*. Philadelphia, Pa.: New Society Publishers, 1983.

Negotiation Journal: On the Process of Dispute Settlement. New York: Plenum Press, 1985.

Newman, Mildred and Berkowitz, Bernard, *How to Be Your Own Best Friend*. New York: Random House, 1973.

Peck, M. Scott, M.D., *The Road Less Travelled*. New York: Simon and Schuster, 1978.

Pogrebin, Letty Cottin, *Stories for Free Children*. New York: McGraw-Hill, 1982.

Prutzman, Priscilla, et al, *The Friendly Classroom for a Small Planet: A Handbook on Creative Approaches to Living and Problem Solving for Children*. Children's Creative Response to Conflict, Box 271, Nyack, N.Y. 10960.

Thomas, Marlo, *Free to Be You and Me*. New York: McGraw-Hill, 1974.

BOOKS FOR PARENTS AND TEACHERS

Axelrod, R., *The Evolution of Cooperation*. New York: Basic Books, 1984.

Azerrad, Jacob, *Anyone Can Have a Happy Child: The Simple Secret of Positive Parenting*. New York: M. Evans and Co., 1980.

Barnet, Richard, *Real Security: Restoring American Power in a Dangerous Decade*. New York: Simon and Schuster, 1981.

Bodner, Joan, *Taking Charge of Our Lives: Living Responsibly in a Troubled World*. San Francisco: American Friends Service Committee.

Brand, Stewart, et al, *The New Games Book*. *The New Games Foundation, 1976.

Buscaglia, Leo, *Living, Loving and Learning*. Thorofare, N.J.: Charles B. Slack, 1982.

Carmichael, Carrie, *Non-Sexist Childraising*. Boston, Mass.: Beacon Press, 1977.

Comstock, Margaret, *Building Blocks for Peace*. Philadelphia, Pa.: Jane Addams Peace Association.

Coppersmith, Stanley, *The Antecedent of Self-Esteem*. San Francisco, Calif.: Freedom and Co., 1967.

Crary, Elizabeth, *Kids Can Cooperate*. Seattle: Parenting Press, 1984.

DeMille, Richard, *Put Your Mother on the Ceiling*. New York: Viking Press, 1972.

Dinkmeyer, Dan and McKay, Gary D., *Parents Handbook: Systematic Training for Effective Parenting*. Minn.: American Guidance Service, Inc./Circle Press, 1976.

Dreikurs, Rudolf, *Family Council: The Dreikurs Technique for Putting an End to War Between Parents and Children (and Between Children and Children)*. Chicago: Henry Regnery Co., 1974.

Easterday, Kate Cusick, *The Peaceable Kitchen Cookbook: Recipes for Personal and Global Well-Being*. New York: Paulist Press, 1980.

Elkind, David, *The Hurried Child: Growing Up Too Fast Too Soon*. Reading, Mass.: Addison-Wesley, 1981.

Falk, Richard, et al *Toward a Just World Order*. Colorado: Westview Press, 1982.

Fluegelman, Andrew, ed., *The New Games Book*. Garden City, N.J.: Doubleday, 1976.

Fraiberg, Selma, *Responsive Parenting*. Minn.: AGS.

Freed, Alvyn M., *TA for Tots*. Rolling Hill Estates, Calif.: Jalmar Press, 1973.

Fugitt, Eva. D.: *"He Hit Me Back First!" Creative Visualization Activities for Parenting and Teaching*. Rolling Hills Estates, Calif.: Jalmar Press, 1983.

Goodman, Mary Ellen, *Race Awareness in Young Children*. New York: Collier Books, 1964.

Gordon, Thomas, *Teacher Effectiveness Training*. New York: Peter Weyden, 1970.

Gottlieb, Sanford, *What About the Russians?*. Cambridge, Mass.: STOP, 1982.

Gregg, Richard B., *The Power of Nonviolence*. New York: Greenleaf Books, 1984.

Haessly, Jacqueline, *Peacemaking: Family Activities for Justice and Peace.* New York: Paulist Press, 1980.

Harrison, Marta, et al. *For the Fun of It: Selected Cooperative Games for Children and Adults.* Philadelphia, Pa.: Friends Peace Committee of the Philadelphia Yearly Meeting, 1976.

Hunger Project, *Ending Hunger,* N.Y.: Praeger, 1985.

Jacoby, Susan, *Inside Soviet Schools.* Farrar/Hill and Wang, 1974.

Josephson, Harold, ed., et al, *Biographical Dictionary of Modern Peace* Leaders. Westport, Conn.: Greenwood Press, 1985.

Judson, Stephanie, *A Manual on Nonviolence and Children.* Philadelphia, Pa.: Nonviolence and Children Program of the Friends Peace Committee, 1977.

Katz, Neil H. and Lauyer, John W., *Communication and Conflict Resolution Skills.* Dubuque, Iowa: Kendall/Hunt Publishing Co., 1985.

King, Martin Luther, Jr., *Why We Can't Wait.* New York: Harper and Row, 1963.

Kohl, Herbert, *Growing with Your Children.* Boston, Mass.: Little, Brown and Co., 1978.

Lechner, Bettye, *Empowering Families: A Manual of Experiences for Family Sharing.* St. Paul, Minn.: National Marriage Encounter, 1977.

Lee, Andrea, *Russia Journal.* New York: Random House, 1981.

Lewis, Claudia, *A Big Bite of the World: Children's Creative Writing.* Englewood Cliffs, N.J.: Prentice-Hall, Inc., 1979.

McGinnis, James and Kathleen, *Educating for Peace and Justice.* St. Louis, Mo.: Institute for Peace and Justice, 1981.

McGinnis, James, et al, *Educating for Peace and Justice: Volume 2, Global Dimensions.* St. Louis, Mo.: Institute for Peace and Justice, 1985.

McGinnis, James and Kathleen, *Parenting for Peace and Justice.* Maryknoll, N.Y.: Orbis Books, 1985.

Michaelis, Bill and Dolores, *Learning through Non-Competitive Activities and Play.* 1977.

Orlick, Dr. Terry, *The Cooperative Sports and Games Book.* New York: Pantheon Books, 1978.

Peace Resource Book 1986: A Comprehensive Guide to Issues, Groups, and Literature. Hagerstown, Md.: Ballinger Publishing Co., 1986.

Philbin, Marianne, ed., *The Ribbon.* Asheville, N.C.: Lark Books, 1985.

Rogers, Carl, *Freedom to Learn.* Columbus, Ohio: Charles E. Merrill Publishing Co., 1979.

Satir, Virginia, *Peoplemaking.* Palo Alto, Calif.: Science and Behavior Books, Inc., 1972.

Schmidt, Fran, *Creative Conflict Solving for Kids.* Miami Beach, Fla.: Grace Contrino Abrams Peace Ed. Foundation, Inc., 1982.

Shannon-Thornberry, Milo, ed., *The Alternate Celebrations Catalogue.* New York: Pilgrim, 1982.

Sharp, Gene, *The Politics of Nonviolent Action.* Boston, Mass.: Extending Horizon Books, 1973.

Shipler, David K., *Russia: Broken Idols, Solemn Dreams.* New York: Penguin Books, 1985.

Stanford, Barbara, *Peacemaking.* New York: Bantam Books, 1976.

Sweeney, Duane, ed., *The Peace Catalog: A Guide Book to a Positive Future.* Press for Peace, 1984.

Tolley, Howard, *Children and War: Political Socialization to International Conflict.* New York: Teachers College Press, 1973.

Wein, Barbara, J. ed., *Peace and World Order Studies.* New York: World Policy Institute, 1984.

Weinstein, Matt and Goodman, Joel, *Playfair: Everybody's Guide to Non-competitive Play.* California: Impact Publishers, 1980.

Wilt, Joy and Watson, Bill, *Relationship Builders.* Waco, Texas: Word Assoc., 1978.

Woolcome, David and Gordon, David, *Peace Child: A Study Guide for Schools.* Washington, D.C.: Peace Child Foundation, PO Box 33168.

CHILDREN'S BOOKS

Alexander, Lloyd, *The King's Fountain.* New York: Harper, 1971.

Bauman, Elizabeth, *Coals of Fire.* Herald Press, 1954.

Bishop, Clarie Hutchet, *Twenty and Ten.* New York: Viking, 1952.

Bolognese, Don, *Once Upon A Mountain.* Lippincott, 1967.

Boylston, Helen, *Clara Barton, Founder of the American Red Cross.* Eau Claire: E.M. Hale, 1955.

Charters, Janet and Forman, Michael, *The General.* New York: E.P. Dutton, 1961.

Clayton, Ed, *Martin Luther King, the Peaceful Warrior.* Englewood Cliffs: Prentice-Hall, 1968.

Coerr, Eleanor, *Sadako and the Thousand Paper Cranes.* New York: G. P. Putnam, 1977.

Cooney, Barbara, *Miss Rumphius.* New York: Viking Press, 1952.

Crippen, David, *Two Sides of the River.* Abingdon, 1976.

De Conde, Alexander, *Decisions for Peace.* New York: G.P. Putnam, 1970.

DeCosse, Paula, *The Children's Whole Future Catalogue.* New York: Random House, 1980.

Duvoisin, Roger, *Snowy and Woody.* New York: Knopf, 1979.

Duvoisin, Roger, *The Happy Hunter.* New York: Lathrop, Lee and Shepard, 1962.

Eaton, Jeanette, *Gandhi: Fighter Without a Sword.* New York: Willam Morrow, 1950.

Epstein, Sam and Beryl, *Harriet Tubman, Guide to Freedom.* New York: Dell, 1975.

Gallomb, Julius *Albert Schweitzer, Genius in the Jungle.* New York: Vanguard Press.

Goodsell Jane, *Eleanor Roosevelt.* New York: Crowell, 1970.

Greenfield, Eloise, *Rosa Parks.* New York: Crowell, 1973.

Harrison, Deloris, ed., *We Shall Live in Peace: The Teachings of Martin Luther King, Jr.* New York: Hawthorne Books, 1968.

Hamanda, Hirusuke, *The Tears of the Dragon.* New York: Parents Magazine Press, 1967.

Hoban, Russell, *The Little Brute Family.* New York: MacMillan, 1966.

Jampolsky, Gerald, *Children as Teachers of Peace.* Celestial Arts, 1982.

Lawson, Don, *Ten Fighters for Peace.* New York: Lothrop, 1971.

Leaf, Munro, *The Story of Ferdinand.* New York: Viking Press, 1936.

Lobel, Anita, *Potatoes, Potatoes*. New York: Harper, 1967.
McKee, David, *Two Admirals*. Boston, Mass.: Houghton, 1977.
Meriweather, Louise, *Don't Ride the Bus on Monday: The Rosa Parks Story*. Englewood Cliffs, N.J.: Prentice-Hall, 1973.
Meyer, Elizabeth P. *Fredrick Douglas, Boy Champion of Human Rights*. Childhood of Famous Americans Series.
Milleander, Dhorothula H., *Martin Luther King, Boy With a Dream*. Childhood of Famous Americans Series.
Moeri, Louise, *Downwind*. New York: E.P. Dutton, 1984.
Oppenheim, Joanne, *Sequoyah, Cherokee Hero*. Mahway, N.J.: Troll Associates, 1979.
Ringi, Kjell, *The Stranger*. New York: Random House, 1968.
Russian Coloring Book. Students of Friend's School, 5114 N. Charles St., Baltimore, Md., 21210. 1978.
Sanchez, Garcia, *La Nina Invisible*. Wensell, 1968.
Seuss, Dr. *The Butter BAttle Book*. New York: Random House, 1984.
Shedd, Charlie, *Promises to Peter: Building a Bridge from Parent to Child*. Waco, Texas: Word Assoc., 1970.
Tree, Marie Housman, *Albert Einstein, Young Thinker*. Childhood of Famous Americans Series
Ungerer, Tomie, *Zeralda's Ogre*. New York: Harper, 1967.
Wagoner, Jean Brown, *Jane Addams, Little Lame Girl*. Childhood of Famous Americans Series.
Wahl, Jan, *How the Children Stopped the Wars*. New York: Farrar, Straus, Giroux, 1969.
Williams, *Come To Russia*. New York: Warwick, 1979.
Wondriska, William, *The Tomato Patch*. New York: Holt, 1964.

RECORDS AND TAPES

Free to Be You and Me, Ms. Foundation, New York, N.Y.
"No More" Record Album Series (No More Feeling Weird, No More Feeling Cheated, etc.) Word Inc., Waco, Texas 76710
"On the Radio," by Jonathan Sprout, Sprout Records, P.O. Box 188, Morrisville, PA 19067. Songs reflect acceptance, friendship, and just plain fun.
"We All Live Together" Album Series, Youngheart Records, Los Angeles, Calif.
Two Hands Hold the Earth by Sarah Pirtle (tape) Love of self, humanity, and nature are stressed in songs and stories for children. A Gentle Wind, Box 3103, Albany, NY12203.
Under One Sky and Look to the People by Ruth Pelham (tapes) Songs reflect a vision of world peace, magnificence of the human spirit. Sumitra Productions, Inc., Box U, Charlemont, MA. 01339
We Are One Planet and Honor the Earth by Molly Scott (tapes) Music reflects the connection between humanity and the earth. Sumitra Productions, Inc., Box U, Charlemont, MA 01339
We Are One with Many Voices by Carolyn McDade (tape) Songs stress our interconnectedness: "one earth, one people, one life." Surtsey Publishers, 111 Mt. Vernon Street, Newtonville, MA. 02160

NEWSLETTERS AND PAMPHLETS

Institute for Peace Studies Newsletter
Center for Peace Studies
University of Akron
Akron, Ohio 44325
COPRED Peace Chronicle
University of Illinois
911 West High Street, Room 100
Urbana, Illinois 61801
Communique
Citizens Exchange Council
18 East 41st Street
New York, NY 10017
Peacemaking for Children
Peace Talks
2437 North Grand Blvd.
Milwaukee, Wisconsin 53210
Prospectus: Conflict Resolution in the Community
Community Board Center for Policy and Training
149 Ninth Street
San Francisco, CA 94102
Peace Education Kit
U.S. Committee for UNICEF
United Nations
New York, NY

RESOURCE ORGANIZATIONS

Children of War Program
c/o Religious Task Force
85 S. Oxford St.
Brooklyn, NY 11217
Children's Creative Response to Conflict
Box 217
Nyack, NY 10960
Offers creative conflict reslolution workshops and resource materials.
Citizens Exchange Council (C.E.C.)
118 East 41st Street, 10th Floor
New York, NY 10017
(212) 725-7659
Coordinates educational and cultural exchanges with the Soviet Union for adults and young people.
Consortium for Global Education
40 South Fullerton Avenue
Montclair, NJ 07042
(201) 783-7616
Provides materials and networking on the teaching of global education skills in the schools.
Consortium on Peace Research, Education, and Development (COPRED)
University of Illinois
911 West High Street, Room 100
Urbana, Illinois 61801
(217) 333-2069
Provides peace education and research materials, and an excellent newsletter.

The Crystal Crusade for Peace
P.O. Box 749
Northhampton, MA 01060
(413) 584-8833 or (212) 260-1713
A network dedicated to the goal that: "Peace will be a reality for all the human family everywhere on earth."

Educators for Social Responsibility (ESR)
23 Garden Street
Cambridge, Mass. 02138
(617) 492-1764
Provides resources and programs on the teaching of peace for all grades.

Foundation for P.E.A.C.E
P.O. Box 244
Arlington, VA 22210
(703) 528-2758

Friends Peace Education and Resource Center
1515 Cherry Street
Philadelphia, PA 19102
(215) 241-7220
A resource library which provides a wide variety of teaching materials on peace education and global understanding.

Gandhi Foundation
273 E. 10th St.
New York, NY 10009
(212) 529-3680

The Hunger Project
P.O. Box 789
San Francisco, CA 94101

Intercommunity Center for Justice and Peace
20 Washington Square No.
New York, NY 10011

Interhelp
P.O. Box 331
Northampton, MA 01061
(413) 586-6311
An organization dedicated to the promotion of peace, acceptance, and understanding.

International Research and Exchanges Board (IREX)
126 Alexander Street
Princeton, NJ 08540
(609) 683-9500
A clearinghouse for organizations doing education and cultural exchanges.

National Parenting for Peace and Justice Network (NPPJN)
Jim and Kathy McGinnis
Institute for Peace and Justice
4144 Lindell Blvd.
St. Louis, MO 63108
(314) 533-4443
A national ecumenical network focusing on parenting for peace and justice.

Neve Shalom
225 W. 34th St., Room 918
New York, NY 10122
(212) 944-7094
An Arab-Jewish Cooperative settlement and school for peace.

Peace Education Network
324 Madeline Drive
Pasadena, CA 91105
Connects people teaching at the pre-collegiate level who are working on peace education.

Partners in Peacemaking
120 Finderne Avenue
Bridgewater, NJ 08807
(201) 231-1181
An education and resource organization which provides curricula and projects to develop peace, acceptance, and cooperation.

San Francisco Study Group for Peace and Disarmament
2735 Franklin St.
San Francisco, CA 94123

FIELD STUDY

Learning the Skills of Peacemaking has a successful classroom "track record" supporting its publication. A field study conducted during the 1985-86 school year produced some "hard" data to back up the "soft" data collected from parents, teachers, and students since the program was originally conceived in 1983. The results from the field demonstrate that *Learning the Skills of Peacemaking:*

- significantly improves student self-concept

- increases students' awareness of alternative ways to resolve interpersonal conclict

- motivates students to express greater care for one another, for humanity, and for the environment

The program was so successful that two local legislators proposed a bill before the New Jersey State Assembly requesting funds for teacher training in *Learning the Skills of Peacemaking.* When the bill passes, teachers will be able to attend college classes and receive Master credits for their course work. Our vision is that, out of this pilot program, other states will also legislate funding for teacher training in *Learning the Skills of Peacemaking.* The success of the program does not depend on teacher training; however, the training would be an added bonus.

THE PILOT STUDY

During the 1985-86 school year, Dr. Harold Sobel of Queens College in New York and I conducted a field study to measure the validity and usefulness of *Learning the Skills of Peacemaking.* Under the guidance of the National Foundation for the Improvement of Education, we designed a pilot study involving 345 elementary school students in seven different public schools in New Jersey and New York. We selected the schools carefully in order to obtain a mix of students from differing socio-economic and ethnic backgrounds. We selected two schools in the heart of one of New Jersey's poorer inner-cities; two schools in a suburban middle to upper-middle class area; one school in a rural district; one school in a poor to middle class district; and two schools in New York's Brooklyn school district. Of the 345 participating students, 187 were boys and 158 were girls. There were 260 white students, 83 black, 16 Hispanic, 6 Asian; 16 students were handicapped.

The children's grade levels ranged from pre-kindergarten to sixth grade. We selected one pre-kindergarten class; one regular kindergarten; one first grade; two inter-aged first/second grades; three regular second grades; five third grades; three fourth grades; one inter-aged fourth/fifth grade class of neurologically impaired students; two regular fifth grades; one sixth grade; and one non-graded class of perceptionally impaired students. Socio-economically, 252 students were rated middle-class, 74 lower class, and 19 upper class.

The 20 participating teachers attended work-shops of varying lengths: 8 teachers attended a 2-day workshop, 11 teachers attended a 1-day workshop, and one teacher did not attend a workshop but was briefed by a colleague.

SELF-ACCEPTANCE: THE CORNERSTONE OF PEACEMAKING

Since self-acceptance is the cornerstone of peacemaking, the pilot study measured changes in self-concept with a standardized test administered at the beginning and end of the school year. The Inferred Self-Concept Scale was administered in the fall of 1985. This test measures various areas of self-concept such as whether or not the children enjoy working with others, feel self-confident, think the teacher likes them, etc.

Another crucial measure of the success of the program concerned observations of and dialogues with the participating teachers. Dr. Sobel visited every class at least once, and I visited most of the classes as well. We followed up our visits with conferences and phone calls. We wanted to see what worked, what didn't work, and how the children were responding as the year progressed. Each participating teacher kept a log in which he or she recorded when the peacemaking lessons were taught and class reactions to the lessons. The majority of the teachers taught one to two lessons each week throughout the school year.

Some representative comments from participating teachers were:

"My class was neurologically impaired and when they started school their sense of self was very poor. Their self-esteem definitely improved out of the program, and so did their acceptance of the people around them."

"By the end of the year the overall attitude that existed around the kids was 'Let's not fight. Let's find some other way to work it out.' In the beginning of the year they fought all the time."

"The kids really looked forward to doing the peacemaking program each week because it was relevant to our lives."

"The children no longer felt it was necessary to fight physically. The program improved their group relationships."

"In our school we taught the cafeteria and playground aides to do what we were doing, particularly the Win/Win process. It really helped."

In the beginning of the year the boys in particular had the attitude of 'Me first, and the heck with everyone else!' Toward the end, the attitude shifted to 'Let's work together.' They became very encouraging toward one another."

"I noticed an increasing awareness of mutual respect toward other students, the teachers, and the environment. There emerged a peaceful way of operating that I would call upon to resolve conflicts and promote a peaceful classroom."

"The program has helped me to become more aware of my own actions. It has made me rethink my style from authority figure to mediator. It also helped the kids solve their own problems."

"*Learning the Skills of Peacemaking* helped bring into focus the understanding that peace begins with me. It has brought all of my positive learning skills into focus. I realize that I'm responsible for everything I stand for in life."

"Through *Learning the Skills of Peacemaking* we are helping the children realize that they have choices. They have the power to make their own decisions, and they are learning to take responsibility for their actions."

AUTHOR INFORMATION

Naomi Drew is former Executive Director of Partners in Peacemaking, a peace education and resource organization originally administered by the National Foundation for the Improvement of Education. Partners in Peacemaking creates public school programs that foster interpersonal cooperation and understanding.

Ms. Drew has taught elementary school for sixteen years. She developed and piloted *Learning the Skills of Peacemaking*. Over the past eleven years, she has addressed thousands of educators, parents, and community groups in the area of peacemaking, conflict resolution, and self-esteem. She currently teaches at Cambridge School in South Brunswick, New Jersey. She has been teaching for nineteen years.

Ms. Drew has conducted workshops for the Association for Supervision and Curriculum Development, the New Jersey School Board Association, the New Jersey Education Association, the New Jersey State Department of Education (Monmouth County), the Governors's School, the New York Council on Early Childhood Education, the New Jersey State Professional Guidance and Counselors Association, Gifted and Talented Association, the New Jersey State Association of Kindergarten Educators, the League of Women Voters, and many school districts. Her work has been the topic of numerous radio, television, and newspaper reports.

Ms. Drew's work in teaching the skills of peacemaking has served as a vehicle to bring this crucial area of studies into schools throughout the United States. Her program was the subject of a bill in the New Jersey State Legislature to provide state funding for teacher training in peacemaking skills.

Ms. Drew visited the Soviet Union in April, 1985. At that time she presented a draft of *Learning the Skills of Peacemaking* to educators in Moscow and Tbilisi (Soviet Georgia).

The book has been translated into Portuguese, Russian, Romanian and Hungarian and is bringing peacemaking skills to children around the world.

Partners in Peacemaking has completed work on a series of international youth art exhibitions showing children's visions of a world at peace. In May, 1986, Ms. Drew and her colleagues at Partners in Peacemaking presented an overview of their organization's goals and accomplishments to members of the President's staff at the White House.

Ms. Drew was awarded the Prestigious Governor's Teachers Grant in 1988.

PRACTICE prevention rather than intervention!
DEVELOPING positive self-esteem is our best weapon against drug and alcohol abuse!

Project Self-Esteem, Expanded (Gr. K-6)

Innovative parent involvement program. Used by over 2000 schools/400,000 participants. Teaches children to repect themselves and others, make sound decisions, honor personal and family value systems, develop vocabulary, attitude, goals and behavior needed for successful living, practice responsible behavior and avoid drug and alcohol use.

Sandy McDaniel & Peggy Bielen

0-915190-59-1, 408 pages, **JP-9059-1 $39.95**
8½ x 11, paperback, illus., reprod. act. sheets

Esteem Builders (Gr. K-8)

Teach self-esteem via curriculum content. Best K-8 program available. Uses 5 building blocks of self-esteem (security/ selfhood/ affiliation/ mission/ competence) as base. Over 250 grade level/curric. content cross-correlated activities. Also assess. tool, checklist of educator behaviors for modeling, 40 week lesson planner, ext. bibliography and more.

0-915190-53-2, 464 pages, **JP-9053-2 $39.95**
8½ x 11, paperback, illus.,reprod. act. sheets

Michele Borba, Ph.D.

NEW

Self-Esteem: The"Affiliation" Building Block (Gr. K-6)

Making friends is easy with the activities in this thoroughly researched book. Students are paired, get to know each other, produce a book about their new friend, and present it in class. Exciting activities help discover commonalities. Great self-esteem booster. Revised after 10 years of field testing. Over 18 activities.

C. Lynn Fox, Ph.D.

0-915190-75-3, 128 pages, **JP-9075-3 $14.95**
8½ x 11, paperback, illustrations, activities

NEW

6 Vital Ingredients of Self-Esteem: How To Develop Them In Your Students (Gr. K-12)

Put self-esteem to work for your students. Learn practical ways to help kids manage school, make decisions, accept consequences, manage time, and discipline themselves to set worthwhile goals...and much more. Covers developmental stages from ages 2 to 18, with implications for self-esteem at each stage.

0-915190-72-9, 208 pages, **JP-9072-9 $19.95**
8½ x 11, paperback, biblio., appendices

Bettie B. Youngs, Ph.D.

Feelings Alphabet: An Album of Emotions from A to Z (Gr. Pre.K-4)

Watch self-awareness and self-acceptance grow page-by-page as you use this delightful book. Teaches children the alphabet and about themselves and their feelings. Once they can express their feelings, they can learn. And when they learn, they feel good about themselves. An enabling book. "One-of-a-kind" photos.

Judy Lalli, M.S.

0-915190-82-6, 72 pages, **JP-9082-6 $7.95**
6 x 9, paperback, 33 B/W photos

Learning The Skills Of Peacemaking: Communicating/Cooperation/Resolving Conflict (Gr.K-8)

Help kids say "No" to fighting. Establish WIN/WIN guidelines for conflicts in your classroom. Over fifty lessons: peace begins with me; intregating peacemaking into our lives; exploring our roots and interconnectedness. Great for self-esteem and cultural diversity programs.

0-915190-46-X, **JP-9046-X $21.95**
8½ x 11, paperback, illus.,reprod. act. sheets

Naomi Drew, M.A.

REVISED

He Hit Me Back First: Self-Esteem Through Self-Discipline (Gr. K-8)

By whose authority does a child choose right from wrong? Here are activities directed toward developing within the child an awareness of his own inner authority and ability to choose (will power) and the resulting sense of responsibility, freedom and self-esteem. 29 separate activities.

Eva D. Fugitt, M.A.

0-915190-64-8, 120 pages, **JP-9064-8 $12.95**
8½ x 11, paperback, appendix, biblio.

NEW

You & Self-Esteem: The Key to Happiness & Success (Gr. 5-12)

Comprehensive workbook for young people. Defines self-esteem and its importance in their lives; helps them identify why and how it adds or detracts from their vitality; shows them how to protect it from being shattered by others; oulines a plan of action to keep their self-esteem positive. Very useful.

0-915190-83-4, 128 pages, **JP-9083-4 $14.95**
8½ x 11, paperback, biblio., appendices

Bettie B. Youngs, Ph.D.

Self-Awareness Growth Experiences (Gr. 7-12)

Over 593 strategies/activities covering affective learning goals and objectives. To increase: self-awareness/self-esteem/social inter-action skills/problem-solving, decision - making skills/coping ability/ ethical standards/independent functioning/ creativity. Great secondary resource. Useful in counseling situations.

V. Alex Kehayan, Ed.D.

0-915190-61-3, 224 pages, **JP-9061-3 $16.95**
6 x 9, paperback, illus., 593 activities

Unlocking Doors to Self-Esteem (Gr. 7-12)

Contains curriculum content objectives with underlying social objectives. Teach both at the same time. Content objectives in English/Drama/Social Science/Career Education/ Science/Physical Education Social objectives in Developing Positive Self-Concepts/ Examining Attitudes, Feelings and Actions/Fostering Positive Relationships.

0-915190-60-5, 224 pages, **JP-9060-5 $16.95**
6 x 9 , paperback, illus., 100 lesson plans

C. Lynn Fox, Ph.D. & Francine L. Weaver, M.A.

ORDER FROM: Jalmar Press, 45 Hitching Post Drive, Bldg. 2, Rolling Hills Estates, CA 90274-5169
CALL TOLL FREE — 800/662-9662. IN CALIF. CALL COLLECT — 213/547-1240. FAX — 213/547-1644

6/91

DISCOVER materials for positive self-esteem.
CREATE a positive environment in your classroom or home by opening a world of understanding.

DISCOVER books on self-esteem for kids.
ENJOY great reading with Warm Fuzzies and Squib, the adventurous owl.

20 YEARS
AWARD WINNING
PUBLISHER

Alvyn Freed, Ph.D.

TA for Tots Coloring Book (Gr. PreK-3)

Come to OK Land and paint all your TA for Tots friends happy with your trusty crayons or water colors. Constructive, creative coloring fun. Color the Warm Fuzzy. Warm Fuzzies are warm feelings — feelings of being OK and being loved. Helps show kids that taking care of their feelings is OK! Great for rainy day activities for your charges.

0-915190-33-8, 24 pages, **JP-9033-8 $1.95**
11 x 8½, saddle-stitched, illustrated

REVISED

TA for Tots (and other prinzes) Revised (Gr. PreK-3)

Over 500,000 sold. New upright format. Book has helped thousands of young children and their parents to better understand and relate to each other. Helps youngsters realize their intrinsic worth as human beings; builds and strengthens their self-esteem. Simple to understand. Great for parents and other care givers.

0-915190-73-7, 144 pages, **JP-9073-7 $14.95**
8½ x 11, paperback, delightful illustrations

Alvyn Freed, Ph.D.

Alvyn Freed, Ph.D.
& Margaret Freed

TA for Kids (and grown-ups too) (Gr. 4-9)

Over 250,000 sold. An ideal book to help youngsters develop self-esteem, esteem of others, personal and social responsibility, critical thinking and independent judgment. Book recognizes that each person is a unique human being with the capacity to learn, grow and develop. Hurray for TA! Great for parents and other care givers to use to use in school or at home.

0-915190-09-5, 112 pages, **JP-9009-5 $9.95**
8½ x 11, paperback, illustrations

TA for Teens (and other important people) (Gr. 8-12)

Over 100,000 sold. The book that tells teenagers they're OK! Provides help in growing into adulthood in a mixed-up world. Contrasts freedom and irresponsibility with knowing that youth need the skill, determination and inner strength to reach fulfillment and self-esteem. No talking down to kids.

0-915190-03-6, 258 pages, **JP-9003-6 $18.95**
8½ x 11, paperback, illustrations

Alvyn Freed, Ph.D.

Claude Steiner, Ph.D.

The Original Warm Fuzzy Tale (Gr. PreK —Adult)

Over 100,000 sold. The concept of Warm Fuzzies and Cold Pricklies originated in this delightful story. A fairy tale in every sense, with adventure, fantasy, heroes, villians and a moral. Children (and adults, too) will enjoy this beautifully illustrated book. Great for parents and other care givers.

0-915190-08-7, 48 pages, **JP-9008-7 $7.95**
6 x 9, paperback, full color illus.

Moths & Mothers/Feathers & Fathers The Story of Squib, The Owl, Begins (Ages 5-105)

Heartwarming story of a tiny owl who cannot fly or hoot as he learns to put words with his feelings. He faces frustration, grief, fear, guilt and loneliness in his life, just as we do. Struggling with these feelings, he searches, at least, for understanding. Delightfully illustrated. Ageless.

0-915190-57-5, 72 pages, **JP-9057-5 $7.95**
8½ x 11, paperback, illustrations

Larry Shles, M.A.

Larry Shles, M.A.

Hoots & Toots & Hairy Brutes: The Continuing Adventures of Squib, The Owl (Ages 5-105)

Squib, who can only toot, sets out to learn how to give a mighty hoot. Even the owl-odontist can't help and he fails completely. Every reader who has struggled with life's limitations will recognize his own struggles and triumphs in the microcosm of Squib's forest world. A parable for all ages.

0-915190-56-7, 72 pages, **JP-9056-7 $7.95**
8½ x 11, paperback, illustrations

Hugs & Shrugs: The Continuing Saga of Squib, The Owl (Ages 5-105)

Squib feels lonely, depressed and incomplete. His reflection in the pond shows that he has lost a piece of himself. He thinks his missing piece fell out and he searches in vain outside of himself to find it. Only when he discovers that it fell in and not out does he find inner-peace and become whole. Delightfully illustrated. Ageless.

0-915190-47-8, 72 pages, **JP-9047-8 $7.95**
8½ x 11, paperback, illustrations

Larry Shles, M.A.

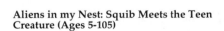

Larry Shles, M.A.

Aliens in my Nest: Squib Meets the Teen Creature (Ages 5-105)

What does it feel like to face a snarly, surly, defiant and non-communicative older brother turned adolescent? Friends, dress code, temperament, entertainment, room decor, eating habits, authority, music, isolation, internal and external conflict and many other areas of change are dealt with. Explores how to handle every situation.

0-915190-49-4, 80 pages, **JP-9049-4 $7.95**
8½ x 11, paperback, illustrations

Do I Have to Go to School Today? Squib Measures Up! (Ages 5-105)

Squib dreads going to school. He day-dreams about all the reasons he has not to go: the school bus will swallow him, the older kids will be mean to him, numbers and letters confuse him, he is too small for sports, etc. But, in the end, he goes because his teacher accepts him "just as he is." Very esteeming. Great metaphor for all ages.

0-915190-62-1, 64 pages, **JP-9062-1 $7.95**
8½ x 11, paperback, illustrations

Larry Shles, M.A.

ORDER FROM: Jalmar Press, 45 Hitching Post Drive, Bldg. 2, Rolling Hills Estates, CA 90274-5169
CALL TOLL FREE — 800/662-9662. IN CALIF. CALL COLLECT — 213/547-1240. FAX — 213/547-1644

6/91